# GROWING UP IN
# CAMBRIDGE

# GROWING UP IN
# CAMBRIDGE
## From Austerity
## to Prosperity

### ALEC FORSHAW

The
History
Press

## Dedication

In memory of my parents, Margaret and Donald Forshaw.

## Acknowledgements

Thanks are due to my brother Roger and my friend John Richens for reading, correcting and contributing to the text, my school geography teacher Peter Bryan for his encouragement, the staff of the Cambridge Collection at Milton Road Library and the Shire Hall, Michael Harrison and Maree Allitt at Kettle's Yard, Sandra Burkett of Cambridge Newspapers, Wayne Boucher of the Cambridge 2000 collection, and to Rodney Dale who told me about Tommy the horse.

First published 2009

The History Press
The Mill, Brimscombe Port
Stroud, Gloucestershire, GL5 2QG
www.thehistorypress.co.uk

© Alec Forshaw, 2009

The right of Alec Forshaw to be identified as the Author
of this work has been asserted in accordance with the
Copyrights, Designs and Patents Act 1988.

British Library Cataloguing in Publication Data.
A catalogue record for this book is available from the British Library.

ISBN 978 0 7524 5004 9

Typesetting and origination by The History Press
Printed in Great Britain

# CONTENTS

# PROLOGUE

Surely, not another book about Cambridge, a place so documented, so recorded, so photographed, so eulogised, and so saturated with writers and their texts; how can one contemplate another?

This is a story of a childhood in Cambridge in the 1950s and '60s, followed by three undergraduate years and three decades of frequent and regular visits until the ties of the parental home were broken.

These are memories set down before they too disappear, and they recall a Cambridge which for many will have faded.

When, as a teenager, I first read Gwen Raverat's *Period Piece - A Cambridge Childhood*, her description of the town and its society seemed like a different world. I cannot hope to emulate the deft charm and eloquence of her writing, but the following reminiscences may interest and amuse a few, and that would be worth the while.

It is said that however long you live, however far you travel, the streets or fields where you played as a child will always be home to you. Though I may never live there again, so Cambridge is for me.

# A FIRST HOME

My parents moved to Cambridge in 1949, two years before I was born, but with my elder brother Roger who was three at the time. They had no roots or previous connections with Cambridge, but came because of employment.

My father, Donald, was trained as a mechanical engineer and, after an unpleasant and nerve-wracking stint in the Royal Navy at the beginning of the war, had been posted out to India, with my mother, where he had worked in Government irrigation projects in the Himalayan foothills in the Punjab. They had returned to England in 1947 following partition and the ensuing violence and disruption. They had come back to Bedford, my mother's home town, where they lived with my formidable grandmother while my father tried to find work.

My father's home town was Wallasey, part of Birkenhead on the Cheshire bank of Merseyside, where his father had worked as a shipping clerk in the docks. When my father left school he had gone to Bedford to train 'on the job' at W.H. Allen & Sons' engineering works who designed and manufactured engines, pumps, tools and the like. He did his technical professional exams at night school.

My mother, Margaret, had been brought up as the eldest of three children by a determined single mother and had gone up to London to work in a florist shop when she left school in 1934, but regularly came home to Bedford at weekends. She met my father at Bunyan Meeting, the non-conformist chapel in the middle of town. Having been raised as a good Presbyterian by his Scottish mother, this was probably the nearest equivalent my father could find in Bedford. They married in 1941, before going out to India.

They came to Cambridge because my father secured a job with the Great Ouse River Board (GORB), shifting his engineering skills from irrigation to drainage and flood protection in the Fens. GORB's offices were in a big Victorian house in Brooklands Avenue, near the other regional Government offices, which at that time were mostly in temporary huts. GORB later became the Great Ouse River Authority, and then part of Anglian Water.

After a year of renting, helped with a loan of £150 from my Bedford grandmother and a mortgage, my parents bought a house, freehold for £450. It was about halfway along the road from the Cambridge to the village of Histon, and part of a small group of mainly 1930s houses, almost a mile from the junction with Huntingdon Road where Murkett's Garage stood on the corner. The house had been called 'Orcombe' by the previous owners or builders, and my parents never thought to change it. At some stage it became No. 320 Histon Road.

This cluster of houses had been built on former orchards, and was still surrounded by market gardens, allotments and farmland. Although it was separate from the built-up part of Cambridge it was just within the 30mph speed limit, and just within the administrative boundary of the town.

Histon Road runs north – south, and pretty straight; good for traffic in a hurry. Orcombe was on the east side, on the south corner of the junction with Roseford Road which was a short cul-de-sac of similar 1930s houses, mainly semis. The houses had been constructed by a local builder, Mr Ford, who named the street after his mother Rose.

Our house was detached, in red brick with a mock-Tudor front gable, brown clay tiles for the roof, and timber casement windows. The house, like its neighbours on that side of the road, was set back behind a generous front garden. The back garden stretched seventy yards, with a hawthorn hedge as the boundary to the pavement along Roseford Road. The back got the morning and early afternoon sun; the front garden, with its gravel drive, lawn and herbaceous border, got the evening light and the sunsets.

The house itself was not as grand as perhaps it sounds. The ground floor had three rooms, a small front sitting room with a window overlooking the front lawn, a smaller rear dining

The front garden at Orcombe, Histon Road, April 1958. (Author's Collection)

room, just big enough for a table, chairs and sideboard, and on the north side, with a window onto the drive, a galley kitchen and a chilly larder. The kitchen had a door onto the side passage. The front door, which we rarely used and was reserved for the postman and special visitors, was on the south side, with a little porch under a lean-to roof leading to a modest hall with slippery, polished red floor tiles. The steep single flight of stairs ran off the hall in the middle of the house, between the front and rear rooms, and arrived at a landing off which were three bedrooms and a bathroom. The front bedroom, above the sitting room, was my brother's. My parents had the rear room over the dining room, sheltered at the back from traffic noise and sunny in the morning. Being in no position to argue, I was allocated the tiny third room at the back, over the kitchen. The bathroom, above the larder, would be described today by silver-tongued estate agents as 'compact'; big enough only for a short cast-iron bath and a toilet alongside. All the bedrooms, surprisingly, had wash-basins, which was considered a great luxury, and certainly eased pressure on the bathroom. The toilet was always called the lavatory, and like most families we had our special words for various things. 'Have you done your "job" yet?' would be demanded through the bathroom door every morning by my mother. My father even referred to dog mess on the pavement as 'Don't tread in those jobs!'

Outside, on the north side, separating front and back, was a black timber garage with a corrugated iron roof and a bike and tool shed in similar ship-lap timber. The shed had the musty smell of string and sacks of potatoes, mingled with drips of oil and petrol from the Suffolk Punch lawnmower, paraffin rags and the sweet tang of last autumn's apples stored in wooden boxes lined with newspaper. The rear dining room had a French window with double doors leading on to a veranda running along the back of the house off which was a brick lean-to outside lavatory. With its concrete floor, flimsy latch door with a big gap at the bottom, and a distinct absence of heating, this was a draughty and freezing retreat, and no place to linger. My father's khaki pith helmet from the Raj hung on a nail on the back of the door.

This in a nutshell, was my home, and was to be so until I went to university.

My house.
My house is a ordinary house made of old red brick. It has black window-frames and the out-side doors are black too. My house has two chimneys. My house is not thatched but it is tiled, and it has reddish tiles. We have not got a television but we've got two wirelesses and we've got two gramophones which are broken. Our house has got a porch, and in the summer we put the bulbs in the porch. I have a bedroom of my own.

*Above:* A seven-year-old's description of home.

*Left:* The back of the house, 1960. (Author's Collection)

# NEIGHBOURS

The house next door was called 'Cheriton', probably also named by the builder who had a fondness for small villages in Devon. It was also detached although only a few feet away and a narrow alleyway from our flank wall. It was designed in a faux Dutch style, gabled at front and back and with a double or broken pitch for the side roofs. The two houses made an odd pair.

Cheriton was let to St John's College, and they used it to house mature graduate students or visiting Fellows with families. We thus had a succession of neighbours from all corners of the globe, which provided a great source of delight and amusement, and occasionally an irritation to my parents, but above all, an eye-opening cosmopolitan education for me and my brother.

Our favourites were the Parrs from Pennsylvania, not only because they stayed for several years, but because their children Stephen and Carol were the same age as my brother and I, and they became lifelong family friends. Their stay in Cambridge was when I was only three or four years old, but Bob Parr frequently returned to England on academic business, usually with his wife Jane in tow. They were generous with their money and would take us out to dinner in exotic places like the Garden House Hotel, or the University Arms whose restaurants my parents would never have been able to afford. Once we went to visit them when they were in Oxford, and they entertained us in their up-market hotel in Woodstock.

By contrast, the Grillos from Nigeria allowed the garden to go to rack and ruin, much to my mother's mortification, and hung out their washing on a Sunday. One side-effect of my parents' stay in India was that they hated the smell of curry and all spicy food. Enough said, but the Chands from Fiji and the Carringtons from Jamaica were the happiest families you could ever meet, always smiling and laughing. The Frasers from Canada were dour, but gardened like troopers.

Our other neighbours were less transient. In the next house after Cheriton were the Barretts, who we had little to do with, except retrieving tennis balls which had flown a long way. Directly across the road was Clive Vale Nursery, a smallholding of glasshouses and neatly cultivated plots

With the Parrs at The Orchard, Grantchester 1961. (Author's Collection)

where Michael and Gillian Dear grew flowers and vegetables for market, and lived in the bay-windowed pale-brick house which fronted the road. They seemed similar in age to my parents, but had no children. Michael was a strong handsome man, always in wellington boots and wearing a checked shirt with sleeves rolled up to the elbow. His mother, known simply as Mrs Dear, lived at the bottom end of Roseford Road. She went to our church, and was my 'church friend', the non-conformist equivalent of a godmother. She was a very quiet, almost timid, lady, and her square bay-windowed house always felt cold and dark. But she gave me Easter eggs and chocolate cigarettes at Christmas, and took some interest in my well-being. She was also a benevolent baby-sitter when, occasionally, my parents went to the theatre.

Next to Dear's Nursery in the first of a pair of semis lived the Stanfords, Harold and Nellie, an elderly couple who rarely ventured out. Nellie however kept a close eye on what was going on in the neighbourhood and whenever we left our house by car, there would be a twitch of the net curtains opposite. Next to them at No.327, or 'Ingleton' as it was called, were the Maskells. Claude and Cyril were brothers and both worked in Chivers' jam factory in Histon, but it was Claude's wife, Marge (short for Marguerite) who ran the show. She was a small, pale, wiry woman, with her hair permed white as snow, puffed up into a bouffon. She always wore trousers with hoops under her feet and carpet slippers with pom-poms, and almost invariably had a broom in her hand. She usually addressed me as 'my angel' or 'my sugar lump', which palled with over-use. The two brothers were known to me as 'Uncle Claude' and 'Uncle Cyril', but Marge was always 'Mrs Maskell'.

Every morning, after Cyril's Robin Reliant had chugged off to Chivers, she swept the concrete drive and then the pavement in front of the house. Cyril was not prone to exercise, and his ample frame easily filled his three-wheeler. Claude was leaner and cycled to work, smoking or sucking his pipe en route. Marge kept her men strictly under control, which allowed her to devote most of her attention to Susan, her pet miniature poodle, equally bleached, pampered and be-ribboned, a small version indeed of her mistress. Her darling dog had no brain but a persistent yap, which maddened everyone except Marge. Susan's staple diet appeared to be sugar lumps.

On the other corner with Roseford Road lived the Gees, in a very similar house to ours. They were Jewish. Harry Gee had come from Germany in the early 1930s, settled in Cambridge and ran an electrical shop at No.94 Mill Road. They kept themselves to themselves, particularly Mrs Gee (Priscilla) and their single son, who were rarely seen outside or in the street. I didn't understand remotely what being Jewish meant, except that my mother once confided in me that they had changed or abbreviated their surname from Goldstein 'to avoid drawing attention'. We didn't have much to do with them until my brother became interested in electronics. Some of the cast-offs of Mr Gee's business regularly spread into their front garden, which my mother thought 'lowered the tone', but they became a useful source of components or spare parts for the various radios or circuits which my brother was making or mending.

Immediately beyond the Gees lived Alderman Howard Mallet, an elderly red-faced gentleman with a fine grey walrus moustache, and his wife Ethel, neither of them ever seen outdoors without a hat. He had been a town councillor for years (in fact since 1945), and in 1954-55 he had his year as mayor. We got quite used to the mayoral limousine, a black Bentley, complete with the coat of arms crest on the bonnet, arriving to pick him up in his red robes, tricorn hat and gold chain, and to seeing his picture in the *Cambridge Daily News*. I imagined that all mayors, including 'Mr Mayor' in *Toy Town*, looked like Mr Mallet. It added a brief air of distinction to our little group of houses, although I don't think he much liked little boys pedalling along the pavements on their tricycles outside his house. Nor did the two ladies who lived in No.312. This was a big, rather forbidding house, older than all the others in our little group, and called by us the 'White House' because its Burwell bricks had been so painted.

At the bottom of our back garden, the first house in Roseford Road was occupied by the Sussums, a retired couple who had lived in Cambridge all their lives. My main contact with them was knocking on their front door to ask for access to find balls which had been hit over the close-boarded fence into their back garden. Mr (Ted) Sussum was always sympathetic, having played minor county cricket for Cambridgeshire in the 1920s, and apparently as a boy had played with the legendary Jack Hobbs when he had returned to his home town from his adopted Surrey to play in a charity match. Ted was also the great-grandson of George Sussum, who famously took nine wickets for fourteen runs playing for Cambridge Town against the university, captained by the Earl of Sandwich in 1831. When I was twelve, and more passionate about cricket than anything else, Ted Sussum gave me two of his old bats, never having had children of his own. How I treasured them, and under my father's guidance carefully cleaned and treated them with linseed oil every spring. Sadly one of them developed wood-worm, but the other to this day still has its moments of glory on a Cornish beach.

A couple of doors further down was the Smith family. The father, Harry, worked in the Ministry of Agriculture, Fisheries and Food, and had common interests with my father. Like my mother, Iris was a housewife, and there were two boys, Michael and David, a year older and younger than me. Michael became a good pal and playmate, although we didn't go to the same school. When I was eight they moved away to Harrogate and although I once went to stay with them during an Easter holiday, our two families lost touch, apart from Christmas cards. The last I heard of Michael was that he had dropped out of sixth-form at school and had joined what my mother described as a 'pop group'.

My mother's closest neighbourly confidante was Mrs Hobson, who lived halfway down Roseford Road where the narrow carriageway slightly widened to allow for vehicles to pass or turn. Her house had a pine tree in the front garden in which lived an owl whose nocturnal calls were regular and familiar. Mrs Hobson was a very self-contained, kind and sensible lady. She gave us chocolate biscuits and introduced us to the owl pellets under the tree which we eagerly took to school for dissection to reveal the tiny bones of mice.

I'm sure I knew the names of other neighbours, but they left little impression on my memory bank. There were no great dramas or 'neighbours from hell'. Most people in our compact little cluster of houses kept their own company, polite and well-behaved, living quiet lives in a quiet corner of Cambridge.

## TRADESMEN

Our house was about three miles from the town centre and although there was a small parade of shops halfway up Histon Road, beyond Gilbert Road, we were grateful for the various salesmen who called or passed by.

Our milk came from the Home Farm Dairy in Histon and until 1958 was horse-drawn. The clink of milk bottles as the cart stuttered along Roseford Road at seven o'clock every morning was a frequent and familiar alarm clock for me in my back bedroom. The horse was old, blinkered and passive, never moving faster than a plod, but seemingly content with its nose-bag of oats and bran. Tony, the milkman, was by contrast cheery and sprightly, with a stereotypical whistle of tuneless monotony which unsettled even the blackbirds.

We had silver-top bottles and my mother always carefully poured off the top inch of yellow cream into a separate jug. She also collected the horse droppings in the street to put on the roses in the garden. I didn't know at the time whether the horse had died or been put out to pasture, but the new electric milk float with its whining motor and squeaking brake seemed to be a radical change. Sadly it didn't improve Tony's whistling.

Several times a week a Hovis baker's van would stop outside on Histon Road and the driver would come and knock on our side door, My mother would always buy a large brown loaf. On Thursdays there was a well-stocked fish van, and we were probably one of its early stops as it trundled out to Histon and the villages beyond. The fish man didn't come to the house, but had a hand bell to alert the neighbourhood. As a child I often wondered where the fish came from; we were a long way from the sea, and the River Cam always seemed an unlikely source.

Our house depended on coal for heating, with an open fire in the front room and an enclosed fire in the dining room which also heated the hot water. The coalman was ordered through Underwoods hardware shop and came several times a year, a shifty character with filthy hands, smudges of black on his face and a greasy black cap perched on his mop of tousled black hair. His open lorry had flaps at the side so that he could ease the grey sacks onto his back, and then half run, half stagger up our gravel drive to the corrugated iron coal bunker beside the garage. He spoke with a gruff mutter, and I made sure I kept out of his way.

The rag and bone man was even shiftier, and he used a short whip to urge his pony to a trot. 'Any old iron?' was his cry, but he seemed grateful to take anything. He was so thin and poorly dressed that I assumed that the rags and bones applied to him.

Our favourite caller was Mr Wiseman. He ran a market garden in Cottenham, north of Histon, where he grew potatoes, carrots, turnips, cauliflowers and cabbages, and on Saturdays he did deliveries around the local villages. He worked long hours, and often didn't come until late in the afternoon or early evening. His veined cheeks were cherry red and he always wore a light brown working coat, cloth cap and woollen gloves with the fingers cut off. He would knock on the door, take my mother's order, then scuttle back to his truck, returning with the vegetables and to take the money. One of his pockets chinked with coins. He always seemed in a hurry and out of breath, and my parents often said that he worked too hard and too late, particularly on dark winter evenings. One day we heard that he had been knocked over by a car on one of his rounds and died from his injuries, which saddened us all.

The dustmen and their smelly cart came on Mondays, a gang of men who my mother described as 'uncouth'. We had a metal bin with a metal lid which made a loud clatter as they threw it on the paving. As if to irritate everyone, they never put the lids back on the bins and usually managed to scatter some rubbish on the road. We did our fair bit of recycling, with a compost heap at the bottom of the garden and a separate pile for the ashes from the fire. We kept paper and cardboard to burn on bonfires, and milk bottles were always washed out and put in the crate for collection. Nothing much came in plastic, so it was only tins or cartons, or uneaten meat and fish bones which went in the bin.

The *Daily Telegraph* and the *Cambridge Daily News* were delivered from the newsagent half a mile away by an ever-changing cast of paper boys. Some would take a diagonal short-cut across the front lawn, leaping the flower bed, and one even forced a way through the boundary hedge with next door in an ill-advised frenzy to speed his round. My mother called him 'a cheeky monkey'.

Less frequent callers included a window cleaner who somehow managed to ride his bike carrying his ladder and pail, and a white-haired lady who only had her own two feet for transport and who sold clothes pegs, buttons, ribbons and reels of cotton. My mother said she was a gypsy and not to be trusted, but she seemed harmless enough to me.

Most exciting was the chimney sweep who had a little Baby Austin van to carry his equipment. On his word we would rush out into the garden to see the brush pushed up on its rods and thrust out above the chimney pots. My mother was less enthusiastic about clearing up the dust afterwards.

Passing ambulances, with their insistently jangly bells, or fire engines with their oscillating major-third sirens were an occasional minor excitement. One October Saturday, returning from the allotments, I was surprised to see a fire engine stopped on the road near our house, and then even more amazed to see thick yellow-brown smoke belching from the chimney and realise that the fire was at our house. In the event it was easily put out, but not until the firemen had made a dreadful mess. It was probably the most alarming thing that ever happened at home.

On Wednesday mornings Mrs Lock came to help my mother with cleaning and housework. She lived half a mile away in Darwin Drive, off Akeman Street, in one of the pale-brick 'homes-for-heroes' Council houses. Mrs Lock was a dumpy cheerful woman who never seemed to stop talking. We didn't have a washing machine, only a sink, wooden wash board and a mangle, no refrigerator, and to begin with not even a Hoover, so she helped with some of the routine chores. She would wash the lino kitchen floor on her hands and knees and polish the hall tiles, but much of the time she would stand and chat, drinking cups of Nescafé or savouring a piece of strong cheddar cheese for elevenses. We all knew that her husband was called Albert, but she never told us that her name was Daisy. She was Cambridge-born and bred, but once admitted to my mother that she'd never ever set foot inside any of the colleges, not even King's College Chapel. 'I've no station there', she said. Such was the division for some between 'town' and 'gown'.

After several years my mother decided that Mrs Lock's output did not justify the money, so we made do for a while without any domestic help, until a neighbour recommended her cleaner. Mrs Sparks was an ungainly, big-boned woman, as taciturn as Mrs Lock had been garrulous, and certainly not one to stand around passing the time of day. She lived in Impington and rode an old-fashioned sit-up-and-beg bicycle, rather like my mother's. Her husband Mr Sparks was a gardener (sadly not an electrician), and he came once or twice to help my father with heavy jobs. He was a mild, simple man, well and truly hen-pecked by his wife. Both of them had lived all their lives in the same village and spoke with a strong Cambridgeshire dialect. Like Mrs Lock, neither of them had ever ventured far. Mr Sparks told me that he'd once been up to London to see Buckingham Palace, but didn't think much of it, hadn't seen the Queen, and thought he'd never go there again.

A Tommy lookalike, beside the Northern bypass. (Author's Collection)

I recently found out that the milk horse which was retired in 1958 was spared from the knacker's yard by a group of local children who had formed the Horse Saving Society. They bought Tommy and his float from Chivers Home Farm Dairy, collected money from jumble sales to feed him, and he ended his days grazing happily in a field behind the Scotsdale Laundry.

# LOCAL ENVIRONS – THE ARBURY ESTATE

I don't know whether my parents knew about the plans to expand Cambridge northwards when they first bought the house on Histon Road. Probably not, because it might have influenced their decision to buy. Certainly it wasn't long into my conscious childhood that the words 'Arbury Estate' became a frequent topic of discussion among my parents and neighbours, and a cause of anxiety and annoyance.

Between our group of houses and Gilbert Road, where built-up Cambridge really started, were allotment gardens, sheltered from the road by high hedges, and beyond them open cornfields. The last building on the corner of Gilbert Road was 'the flats', a two storey white block of apartments in a vaguely 1930s Art Deco style, now known as Langham House. I thought they were called 'flats' because they were rather squat and had a flat roof. Opposite them were a group of single storey pre-fabs, put up after the war, and more allotments before a narrow cinder track which led to the Scotsdale Nurseries and Laundry, tucked away behind trees. Between our little hamlet and the villages of Histon and Impington were some more allotments and then orchards of apple and pear trees belonging to Chivers Jam factory. Near to the beginning of Histon and the splendid old windmill there was a pond and several grass fields with horses grazing.

The short length of Roseford Road beside our house ended in an open bar fence with fields of barley stretching far into the distance, right across to the Milton Road, over a mile away. The fields were divided with scrappy intermittent hedges and occasional trees, probably elms. There was a gap in the fence, handy for dog walkers and others who wanted to ramble around the edges of the fields.

Although my brother and I were dutifully trained in the Highway Code by my parents, and judiciously cautioned about the dangers of crossing the road, the levels of traffic were so low in the 1950s that there was never any great prohibition about venturing out onto the tarmac pavements. My brother, with help from my father, made a series of 'trolleys', which were low-level platforms of simple wooden planks, with four wheels taken off an old pram and the front axle steered by rope reins. You scooted or pushed to gain momentum, and then jumped on.

Langham House – 'the flats' – Histon Road. (Author's Collection)

The last allotments on Histon Road, with the Arbury Estate behind. (Author's Collection)

My pride and joy was my little red tricycle, which had a useful 'boot' on the back, perfect for carrying toys or other important possessions. Our adventure playground was the allotments, a strange world of little huts and sheds with narrow grass paths separating the plots of vegetables and flowers. Some of the plots were abandoned, or so infrequently tended that they appeared so, and these became a place for exploration and secret games. I doubt that my parents ever really knew what we got up to, until one Easter holiday when playing with Michael Smith we managed each to lose a wellington boot in the mud of one particular quagmire, and having hobbled home, had to return with my angry mother who was unable to free them. Not until the evening when my father laid some duckboards across the mud were the boots liberated from the ooze.

The encroachment of the Arbury Estate, which began in 1957, cast a great shadow over the neighbourhood. First to go were the pre-fabs and allotments next to Gilbert Road, followed by the construction of the new main access roads for the new housing development. That autumn the field at the end of Roseford Road remained unploughed after the harvest, and weeds soon sprouted through the stubble. Before long, bulldozers and earth scrapers had moved in, grotesque machines which looked like giant grasshoppers. Hedges and trees were grubbed up into great mounds to be burnt in huge bonfires, the air was thick with the smell of diesel and exhaust fumes and the birds were silenced by the roar of the engines. Draglines and mechanical diggers cut trenches for new drains and sewers, and soon lengths of string were pegged out in straight lines on the bare ground, marking the plots for new houses. The following summer, in the long evenings and at weekends, the building sites became new playgrounds, new places to explore and to play hide-and-seek behind the stacks of red and yellow bricks. My parents too would regularly walk around to check progress, and were horrified by the prospect that Roseford Road, once so quiet and peaceful, would become a major access road for the vast new estate. As it happened, Carlton Way off Gilbert Road, and Arbury Road off Milton Way, became the new main spine roads for the labyrinth of new suburbia. Fortunately Roseford Road was not directly connected through to Alex Wood Road, but it was a tranquil oasis no longer and became a through-route into Perse Way and St Albans Road.

I wondered where all the people who moved into the new houses had come from. My mother said they were 'London overspill', whatever that meant, but it didn't sound very nice.

The Snow Cat public house, now The Grove.

The new shopping centre over on Arbury Road and the new pub with its asymmetric, angular sloping roof became something of a new landmark and talking point. The pub was called the Snow Cat, named in honour of Sir Vivian Fuchs who had recently completed a voyage to the South Pole in the eponymous vehicle. Fuchs lived in Newnham, worked at the Scott Polar Research Institute in Lensfield Road and was something of a Cambridge celebrity. The pub still survives as a curious memorial, although sadly it has changed its name to The Grove.

A new church was built in 1958 in Mansel Way, in a very conservative style which somewhat appeased my parents. Even with its stripy brick, it is a dull affair compared to the modernist Baptist church put up a few years later in Arbury Road. A huge new secondary modern school, The Manor, was built on Arbury Road too, to cater for the new residents.

North of Arbury Road the Kings Hedges development continued the sprawl. Kings Hedges Road, like Roseford Road, had been a dead-end, lined with inter-war semis. Now, in the 1960s, it was opened up into a major through road to connect with Arbury Road and Histon Road, close to where the new Northern bypass was planned and eventually completed in 1978. All the intervening fallow fields were covered with similar terraces of two- and three-storey houses and four-storey blocks of flats. Kings Hedges and New Chesterton, as the Arbury Estate was renamed, brought over 20,000 new residents to Cambridge, an unprecedented expansion which greatly stimulated the town's economy. The increased population brought pressure for change elsewhere, not least in Cambridge's shops and employment. For perhaps the first time the town began to rival the university in its domination of the city.

On the west side of Histon Road it was a similar story, but with even less inspired architecture. Opposite Gilbert Road, a new access road serviced a new estate of bungalows and shoe-box houses, linking through to the older Windsor Road. Scotsdale Nursery, which had become a prototype 'garden centre', moved to Cambridge Road Shelford, where it would expand beyond anyone's imagination. Beyond Dear's Nursery the sprawl continued to join up with Histon. When Michael Dear died suddenly and unexpectedly of a heart attack in 1969, the nursery threw in the towel and was sold for development. The little pond with its bulrushes and green weed, and most of the meadows with the horses, disappeared under the roundabout and earthworks for the Northern bypass.

# SATURDAYS

My father, as was normal in the 1950s and '60s, worked on Saturday mornings. Often he had to go to the GORB depot at Ely where he was in charge of the repair workshop. My junior school, the Perse Prep, also operated on Saturday mornings. Even when Saturdays were completely 'free', during holiday time or when I was at secondary school, the morning was always regarded as a time to 'get things done', such as being made to tidy my room, washing the car, tinkering with the bikes, going to the shops or running errands. There was always an eager anticipation for the afternoon, because as a sports-mad child, that for me was usually the best bit of the whole week.

Saturday lunch would be a hasty affair, usually cold luncheon meat or corned beef and a rudimentary lettuce salad, with cold stewed apples for pudding. This was gobbled down because my eyes were set on Grange Road or Fenner's for the rugby or cricket, depending on the season.

If the weather was fine my father and I would go by bicycle, my father adjusting the saddle and riding my mother's old sit-up-and-beg Humber. If it was wet we might drive to the rugby, or not go at all to Fenner's because rain would have stopped play. On autumn and winter Saturdays, when the rugby match would be finished by four o'clock, my father liked to go choral evensong at King's College Chapel, so we would cycle or stride along Burrells Walk and Garret Hostel Lane to the back door of King's.

In the gathering gloom of winter's dusk, the smoke-blackened interior of the chapel was a murky and wondrous place, full of hushed echoes and flickering candles. But we, or rather my father, were not there for the service but for the short organ recital which traditionally followed directly after at 6.30 p.m. As the choir and Dean retreated there was just time for us to sneak through to sit in the choir, and from there, enclosed in the dark and the carved oak stalls, I would gaze up straining to see the fan vaulting as the mighty organ engulfed our ears. Sometimes there was a visiting celebrity such as Francis Jackson from York Minster or Marcel Duprés from Paris. As a challenge to the recitalist, David Willcocks, who was Director of Music and Fellow of King's College, would provide, unannounced, a theme to be improvised upon, honouring one of the great traditions of church organ music. Once we heard the elderly French organist, André Marchal, who had been born blind and who had been hailed by the great Gabriel Fauré as an unparalleled improviser. His fugal coda seemed to make the whole chapel shake. I could easily believe my father's adage that the tuba stop could be heard two miles away in Grantchester. (In fact this myth probably relates to the Trompeta Real stop on the organ of St John's.) These events were my first introduction to the weird sound-world of Oliver Messiaen, Jean Langlais and Jehan Alain, the architecture of J.S. Bach and the majesty of Vierne and César Franck.

In the winter we would be home in time for a late high tea of toast, perhaps a crumpet for a treat, home-made scones and jam and my mother's 'barn brac', made with sultanas soaked in tea. 'Sports Report' would be on the radio, with its rousing 'Out of the Blue' theme tune and the familiar declension of the football results by John Webster.

In the summer, at Fenner's, we would have taken a picnic tea, to see us through to close of play at 6.30 p.m. If it was a lovely day in high summer my mother might have come too, and we would have made our base camp on a thick, woollen tartan rug spread out on the grass beyond the cinder running track. Here there were tennis courts and the cricket practice nets, and always the chance to have a go if they were not being used by the players or grown-ups.

Saturday evenings were always spent at home, either in the garden if it was light and dry, or indoors if it was dark or damp. Two or three times a year my parents would go to the Arts Theatre, usually to see a serious play on the recommendation of my father's brother, John, who was an actor. They also saw Flanders and Swan in *A Drop of Another Hat* to their great delight. To their credit and good fortune, they did also get to see the groundbreaking Footlights reviews

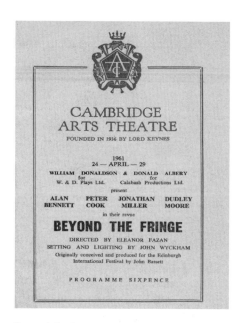

Beyond the Fringe programme.                    King's College Chapel organ recital programme.

with Peter Cook, Jonathan Miller and John Cleese. On those evenings Mrs Dear would baby-sit while Roger and I would persuade her that we could stay up late.

More normally my mother would get on with the ironing, or do some sewing and darning. She made a lot of her own clothes, particularly dresses and skirts, and bought tissue paper patterns through the post, or cut them out of magazines. My father would have his one bath of the week, and change his clothes (which by contrast he did very often). The radio would always be on, with a concert or play reading. My brother would be in his room, fiddling around with something electrical, constructing a complicated crane out of Meccano or making a kit model of the Golden Hind or a Hawker Hunter jet. I would play with my toys in the dining room, in and around the legs of the table, games of make-believe with coloured-glass marbles, wooden bricks, Dinky and Matchbox cars or tin soldiers. When we were older there was always school homework or exam revision to be done, or practising my clarinet.

My father would routinely do the week's accounts on a Saturday evening. This he would do sitting at the little writing bureau in the lounge which had a flap-down lid supported on thin straight wooden arms which slid in and out on either side. In his Boots Scribbling Diary (which without exception he was given for Christmas) he would record every item of expenditure for the week, down to the last penny, all categorised into food, or clothes, or electricity bills, even the sixpence pocket money for my brother and I. He would calculate running totals for the month, and eventually for the year, and work out the surplus or deficit against his salary, which was the family income. It was an extraordinary and obsessive effort. Perhaps it stemmed from his own childhood memories of the pre-war Depression, and paranoia of getting into debt.

Sometimes, when the chores were done and my father felt in the mood, we would play card or board games, either on the dining room table or the little card table with its green baize top and folding legs which lived behind the piano in the lounge. On Saturdays we were usually allowed to stay up later than normal, although everything was relative. My parents never went to bed later than eleven o'clock, and midnight oil did not exist in our house.

*Above:* My father doing his accounts, 1962. (Author's Collection)

*Right:* The accounts – a sample page.

# SUNDAYS

Sundays were as different to Saturdays as chalk is to cheese.

On Sundays only, my parents liked to have a cup of tea in bed before they got up, and until I became a stroppy teenager, I used to deliver this to them. There was something virtuous about being first up, and first downstairs, knowing that you had the kitchen to yourself. Upstairs my parents would be listening to Alistair Cooke's 'Letter from America', while I could enjoy my own silence, the smell of the tea leaves in the cylindrical green-painted tin caddy and the hiss of the gas on the stove as it boiled the kettle.

The tranquillity didn't last long, as the Sunday morning ritual rolled into action. Sundays meant boiled eggs for breakfast and an elaborate and prolonged procedure for getting ready to go to church. This required 'Sunday best' clothes, having one's hair brushed until it shone, and cleaning and polishing shoes until they also shone. My father wore a dark suit and a heavy overcoat if it was cold, and always had his trilby hat. My mother too would always wear a hat to church.

As much as possible of the Sunday lunch was prepared before leaving. This would include shelling peas from their pods into the tin colander, peeling potatoes to be left in a pan of water, and if we were having beef, then making the Yorkshire pudding mixture in a Pyrex bowl. Sunday was the only day of the week we had a roast. The gas oven had to be lit and the joint inserted, on a low flame, so that it would be cooked for our return.

We always went to church by car and usually if it was raining we had someone to pick up on the way. This would often be Walter Hagenbuch who lived on the corner of Histon Road and Gilbert Road. He was young, or at least seemed younger than my parents, blond-haired and blue-eyed, and was always in a lively good humour. His wife was an Anglican and went, I assume by bike, to a different church. Their daughter, Winifred, was a similar age to me, but considered by everyone to be incredibly brainy. She had knocked most of her teeth out when she fell off a swing, so perhaps it was that which drove her to books. Walter Hagenbuch was a well-respected economist and senior tutor at Queens' College, which was handy for my brother later on. On a fraught Sunday morning his cheery presence instantly quelled any bickering in the back seat between me and my brother.

When in 1964 the Hagenbuchs moved away, he to become Professor of Economics and Dean of the University of Kent, we took to picking up Ebenezer Cunningham, who by then was extremely elderly and no longer able to drive the elegant Riley car which stood parked in their drive. He and his equally elderly but disabled wife, Ada, lived in 'Wayside', which seemed to me a rather grand detached house on the corner of Huntingdon Road and Storeys Way. He was a Fellow of St John's College and, according to my reverential father, had worked with Einstein many years ago on mathematical theory. Indeed, he published the first English book on the subject in 1914, *The Principles of Relativity*. He was also an ardent and unpopular pacifist in the Boer Wars and the First World War. The frail Mr Cunningham spoke with a quavering and almost inaudible voice, and usually asked about our schooling. He was always pleased that my brother was good at science. He walked almost impossibly slowly, stooped and bent like his stick, but despite his gait and the fragile tautness of his pale and freckled skin, his eyes always twinkled. When he died in 1977 he was ninety-six years old; he was probably the oldest person I ever knew, born seven years before my grandmother.

Our church was Emmanuel Congregational Church in Trumpington Street, later to become the United Reformed Church. Parking was easy and unrestricted, either in Trumpington Street or round the corner in Mill Lane, although in Trumpington Street itself care was needed not to slip a wheel into the wide-open gulleys between the pavement and the carriageway. These rivulets, fed with the waters from Hobson's Brook, were a great fascination for me and other

Emmanuel United Reformed Church and the old University Press, Trumpington Street.

young children. For one or two magical Sundays in May, they would be pink with the cherry blossom from the trees outside the Fitzwilliam Museum.

Although the service started at 11.00 a.m, we had to get there early because my father was an usher, helping people to their seats and dishing out hymn books. Roger and I would often run down to the Mill Pond to see the river rushing over the weir rather than sit fidgeting in our pew.

Church was a big part of my parents' lives, and they met and made most of their Cambridge friends and acquaintances there. They were devoted non-conformist Christians, but for reasons which were hard to express at the time I never took to it. I found the services tedious and interminable. Like all the other regulars, we had our own particular place, about halfway down on the left-hand side, next to the central aisle, where my father always sat so that he could get out easily to help take the collection. My mother sang in the choir which sat at the front in the apse, near the organ. They would process in front of the minister at the beginning of the service. Mr MacFarlane, who was a senior teacher at the Perse Boys' School and a scout master, sat immediately behind us and deafened us with his booming baritone voice. Opposite us were the Drakes and the Liversleys, the Gibsons and the Disneys (both former caretakers), and in front the Ryland-Smiths, the Connolly family and the Boulinds, and further back still the Allansons, the Lapwoods and the Eaden-Lilleys. The current caretaker, Mr Davies, sat near the front with his hearing aid.

I didn't mind the hymns, although I never much enjoyed communal singing, but I liked the harmonies and changing sounds of the organ in the different verses. Descants were always good. In the prayers and readings I would find the pages in all our hymn books from the number board. The organist was a sprightly lady called Joan Wrycroft, and she had a particular knack of filling time before the start of the service, at the end of hymns and during the collection by doodling in quietly shifting chord sequences.

During the hymn which came before the sermon, the children left for Sunday School, hastening up the aisles to the heavy panelled door in the right-hand corner by the organ, which led to the church hall and other smaller rooms. There we were entertained or otherwise kept amused, the young ones by Maureen Connolly, and the older ones by Bunty Newport. Maureen and her husband had been missionaries in Madagascar, and had exotic tales of Africa. Bunty was a fine pianist, and probably the most effusive and enthusiastic pedagogic musician in Cambridge.

After it was over I would find my father in the vestry, counting the collection, and help shovel the separate piles of coins into little brown bags which my father sealed with a big wet lick.

Sunday lunch was the grandest meal of the week. Roast lamb, pork or beef also meant roast potatoes and gravy, together with the usual overcooked vegetables. Sometimes my parents would have invited a student from church to lunch which kept us all on best behaviour. On festive occasions, or when my uncle John came to visit from London, then there would be a bottle of cider. That, and the decanter of sherry which lived at the back of the bottom shelf of the sideboard and was brought out for special visitors, was the only alcohol in the house.

After lunch my parents always sat in the lounge and drank a pot of tea. Assuming there was no guest they would read *The Sunday Telegraph*, or struggle with the crossword, while listening to 'Gardeners' Question Time'. The dulcet tones of Freddie Grisewood and the idiosyncratic dialects of Bill Sowerbutts, Fred Lodes and Professor Alan Gemill (of Keele University) became an integral and monotonous part of the Sunday ritual. Their very names seem to conjure up water-butts and loads of manure. This postprandial sojourn was a time of frustration for me. 'Let's do something' I would plead.

'Doing something' usually involved a bracing Sunday afternoon walk. Cambridge is not blessed with glorious countryside, so choices were limited. If it was damp we might just go out to Histon, past the windmill and Chivers factory, to the green with its old thatched cottages, and then back on the new road and bridge over the railway. Using the car to go further afield was more fun. Wandlebury Rings and the Roman Road were my favourite, but sometimes we would go to Baits Bite, Clayhythe or Bottisham Lock and trudge along the river banks. On warm, dry summer days, we might take a picnic tea and go as far as Royston Heath or Newmarket Heath, or to Anglesey Abbey at Lode when it was open for the Nurses' Benevolent Fund, but these were special treats. Sometimes we would borrow Walter Hagenbuch's university pass and visit the Botanical Gardens on Trumpinton Road, which were then closed to the public

The Green at Histon, February 1961. (Author's Collection)

The Windmill, Histon.

on Sundays. Least favourite was being dragged around the colleges and their grounds. As a child I hated the 'DO NOT WALK ON THE GRASS' notices, and I had no understanding of the architectural splendours, although I'm sure they left an impression.

On winter evenings my father would sometimes go to play the piano at Castle End Mission, where Dr. Donald Cater presided over the small gathering of the faithful, but the rest of us never went. Later at home there was always talk about dwindling numbers and whether the Mission would survive the redevelopment plans of Cambridge Council. Happily it is still there, now part of a conservation area.

Sundays evenings at home were dull. Alan Keith's 'Your Hundred Best Tunes' would be on the radio, with its hackneyed renditions of Myra Hess's 'Where Sheep May Safely Graze', Kathleen Ferrier's 'Blow the Wind Southerly', 'Greensleeves' and the 'Londonderry Air'. It was a time for self-amusement.

## HOME ENTERTAINMENT

We didn't have a television. While my parents probably thought it was an expensive luxury which they could do without, I think they also believed that a television in the house would discourage my brother and I from reading enough books and distract us from homework. Besides, they were radio addicts, and without conscious choice I became one too.

From the sonorous and reassuring voice of Jack De Manio in the morning to the late night shipping forecast and 'Sailing By', our daily or weekly household routines and timetables were marked, indeed often ruled, by the radio schedule. My parents would obsessively listen to the weather forecast morning and evening before the news. The 'pips' on the hour were always a chance for my father to adjust the clock. I was more fascinated by the 'police messages' where a Mr Arthur Snodgrass, for example, was asked to call Scotland Yard because his mother 'was dangerously ill'. It struck me then as curious that someone might not know that their mother was in such a parlous condition, such was my sheltered existence.

The Home Service was our source of instant news and the first indication to me that there was a wider world. The exploits of Yuri Gugarin and John Sheppard, the death of Dennis Brain, the assassinations of John and Robert Kennedy and the Cuban missile crisis recall visions of our radio set and its extension speaker on the shelf in the dining room, and the hushed sound of concern in my parents' voices.

My earliest memories are of 'Listen With Mother', and the husky deep voice of Daphne Oxenford, and the soothing 'Dolly Suite' on the piano. There was 'Children's Hour' with 'Uncle Mac', and a special edition on Saturday mornings. 'Toy Town' with Larry the Lamb, Mr Grouser and accomplices, were favourites, but also stories such as 'Sparky and the Magic Piano', and the serialisations of *The Lion, the Witch and the Wardrobe*, Arthur Ransome and *Just William* books. Adam Faith's 'Little White Bull', 'Champion the Wonder Horse', and 'the Laughing Policeman' were equally adored, but not by the rest of my family. Later on, 'the Clithero Kid', 'Hancocks Half Hour', 'the Glums', Ken Dodd and his diddymen, 'the Navy Lark', 'the Men From The Ministry' with Richard Murdoch, Derek Guyler and 'Mildred', 'Beyond Our Ken' and 'Round The Horn' were all at one time or another highlights of the week, although the outrageous double-entendres must have passed over my head.

My parents always listened to 'Down Your Way' where Franklin Engelmann interviewed a seemingly random collection of people in a town I'd never heard of, and asked each of them to choose what inevitably amounted to a random and very inconsequential collection of pieces of music. 'Desert Island Discs' with Roy Plomley made more sense to me, and I loved the seagulls in the wonderful Eric Coates theme music. 'Twenty Questions', with its mystery voice and animal-vegetable-mineral classification, 'Round Britain Quiz' and 'My Word' were more cerebral, and my mother would unfailingly marvel at the cleverness of Frank Muir and Dennis Norden as they concocted punning explanations of proverbs or well-known sayings. My parents were immense fans of Victor Borge, Bob Hope, Bob Newhart, Flanders and Swan, Gerrard Hoffnung (with good reason), Joyce Grenfell (more excruciatingly), and Alistair Cooke's 'Letter from America'. Hoffnung's bricklayer monologue never failed to reduce my father to tears of laughter.

For special events, mainly sporting, we did go to our neighbours to watch television. Mrs Dear in Roseford Road always hosted the Boat Race, always seemingly a wet and windy Saturday afternoon in March. Through the commanding commentary of John Snagge I seemed to gain an intimate knowledge of that part of London's riverbank, the tension of the start and the crucial first Middlesex bend, and the thrill of a Cambridge victory, which in the late '50s and early '60s was fortunately more often the case than not.

For the FA Cup Final and the Grand National, which were more 'working class', I would go over the road, usually on my own, to the Maskells. There capacious Cyril would be embedded in his huge armchair, with a bottle or two of brown ale, while Claude would be fretting with his pipe. Mrs Maskell, all the while calling the three of us 'you boys', would endeavour to silence the yapping poodle, and scuttle in and out of the room with biscuits and lurid sickly sweet orange pop for me. My mother would have disapproved, but I loved it, and she never knew.

My father's main passion was rugby, and for the home internationals and the verbose commentary of Bill McClaren, we would go to Mrs Harris, who was the widow of someone my father had known in India. She lived on the corner of Gilbert Road and Carlton Way in a modern house, and with luxurious deep pile carpets and a very big modern telly. What is more, she had chocolate biscuits.

Sir Winston plants a tree at Churchill College (with a glimpse of my legs behind). (Author's Collection)

We all went to Mrs Harris's to see the state funeral of Winston Churchill, the riverside cranes dipping as the barge passed up the Thames, the slow cortege of soldiers and horse-drawn hearse, all in solemn black-and-white. I felt some connection with this, recalling how I had been pushed by my mother to the very front of the crowd who circled the hunched figure of Sir Winston as he shovelled a spade of soil into the tree pit outside the new Churchill College in Storeys Way.

Otherwise my life was television-free, and so all school playground discussion about *Steptoe and Son* or *Coronation Street* were lost on me.

In other respects my father was keen on modern gadgets. Among our friends at church were the Allansons, Douglas and Margaret and their son Christopher, who was about the same age as my brother. My father was a great admirer of Dougie, a dry-witted Yorkshireman who worked at Pye's. He knew everything about the latest hi-fi and cameras, and he inspired my father to buy a tape recorder.

The state-of-the-art reel-to-reel Grundig was a great source of joy for us all. Not only could my father now record and replay to his heart's content all his favourite things off the radio (particularly Gerrard Hoffnung's Oxford Union speeches), but he also used to set up a hidden microphone when friends or relatives came to visit. We would all then derive much amusement from listening to the playback, the strange sound of our voices, the trivia of the conversation and the intrusion of background noises.

We occasionally visited the Allansons' pebble-dashed semi-detached house at No.64 Kings Hedges Road and marvelled at Dougie's slideshows of their exotic holidays in Switzerland. An Ilford Sportsman camera which took colour-slide pictures was also a major acquisition for my father and became an essential piece of equipment on every excursion from the house, not only our holidays in rainy Wales, but visits to relatives and walks around the Cambridge colleges or the American Cemetery. My father spent hours on Sunday evenings labelling every frame and writing a catalogue to record every slide.

Our own slide shows, using a homemade screen fashioned by my mother from cartridge paper and the Kodaslide Home Projector, were fun for us on the first showing, but were remorselessly inflicted on visitors. By the time the Allansons moved to a modern house in Bottisham to escape the escalating development of the Arbury Estate and the transformation of Kings Hedges Road into a major thoroughfare, Dougie had moved on to movie cameras and a hi-fi system with enormous speakers, but my mother dissuaded my father from following suit. Probably they couldn't afford it.

My parents liked playing cards and at an early age, my brother and I were taught simple games such as rummy, twenty-one, and 'old maid', moving on to Newmarket, whist and bezique. Their pride and joy, however, was their mah-jong set, brought back from India, and considered to be the greatest family treasure. I was taught to revere the carved ivory blocks and inlaid shisham counting sticks, and never allowed to consider them as toys, even though building the wall at the start of the game often seemed to me to be the best part.

We also had some of the other commonly available board games, such as Snakes and Ladders, Ludo and a magnificent pre-war Monopoly set with really big bank notes and wooden houses and hotels. Curiously as a child, Waddington's never gave me a very secure knowledge about the geography of London, and later in life I have often pondered how the game could be improved or brought up-to-date. Our most educative game was 'Round Europe', where the object was to 'visit' the capital cities of Europe by collecting cards from a pack. These included air, sea or rail travel tokens for the exact distances and specific modes of transport, the required local currencies, and visas when needed. It's a shame we never actually went to Europe on holiday!

My parents also had another game which they would play with or on visitors who were not 'in the know'. With everyone sitting in a circle, a pair of scissors were passed from one person to the next, either open or closed. They would be passed 'crossed' or 'uncrossed', but the game was that this was nothing to do with the scissors, but depended on whether the passer had their legs crossed or uncrossed. It fooled a surprising number of highly intelligent Cambridge academics, who had perhaps been invited to afternoon tea from church.

Without a television my parents encouraged hobbies, and making things. My father led by example, probably because he enjoyed it more than anyone. We made plaster-of-Paris models and statues, and then painted them; my brother was fiendish with Meccano, and even concocted a little steam engine which ran on methylated spirits. He made Airfix kits of sailing ships and planes with nimble fingers and a fastidious eye for detail, before moving on to electronic circuitry and radio-controlled models..

I had stamp and coin collections, both pump-primed with spares from my father's albums. The letter and postcards we often received from our ex-neighbours scattered around the globe were a windfall.

While my brother had his models and Meccano, I had my train set, a Hornsby O gauge with two clockwork engines and a motley collection of tin carriages and trucks. Lack of space was a problem so no track layout lasted very long, which was a shame because over the years, through various friends we acquired huge amounts of track. In dry summer weather I would lay the track down the garden path and run express trains from the veranda to the compost heap.

My brother making a transistor radio, 1962. (Author's Collection)

We did also read a lot of books. Our local library was the Milton Road branch library in Ascham Road, supplemented in 1966 by the Arbury Court library, and had good children's and adult's sections. I became hooked on Hornblower and other Napoleonic adventures. Sometimes we also went to the central library in Wheeler Street, round the back of the Guildhall, combining it with the less pleasant experience of going to the barber's opposite. I particularly liked looking into the reading room with its magnificent domed roof and its wooden lecterns where old men (keeping warm in the winter) stood to read newspapers whose broadsheets were held in place by brass rods across the central spines. That library too was sadly replaced by a more utilitarian affair in the Lion Yard, although the reading room is preserved as the Tourist Information Centre.

As for pets, my mother didn't like dogs and Histon Road was considered too dangerous for cats. After some pressure, my brother was given a guinea pig which had been 'saved' from a university research lab by one of our next door neighbours. We rather unimaginatively called her the GP. She lived in a little hutch in the shed, or out on the lawn in good weather, but her favourite food was dandelion leaves for which we scoured the neighbourhood verges and hedgerows. GP survived for over four years until her back teeth became too long and she had to be put down. We then experimented with a rabbit, which rapidly trebled in size. This enormous grey buck constantly tried to burrow its way to freedom, and grossly outgrew its cage. We took it back to the breeder in Abingdon.

There were of course seasonal highlights and activities, and not only Christmas, which I describe elsewhere. Birthdays, Shrove Tuesday and Mother's Day all had their special flavour. At Easter we painted our eggs before boiling them for breakfast, and had hollow milk-chocolate eggs whose silver foil wrappers were gingerly removed and smoothed out for safe keeping. Halloween had not yet become a British event but Bonfire Night was a big occasion. Usually the Smiths in Roseford Road had a firework party and we would take our contributions of sparklers and Roman candles, all bought from the newsagent up at the shops opposite Akeman Street. My parents thought that rockets were dangerous and vetoed them. On the year when we had fireworks at home, one of the Catherine Wheels nailed to the rose pergola broke free and set the hedge on fire, all of which fuelled my parents' apprehension. My brother's birthday closely preceded Guy Fawkes night, and several times he was given indoor fireworks as a present. I never thought they were much good. Whatever their genteel charms, the lasting impression was the smell rather than the pyrotechnics.

# CHRISTMAS

When I was too young to remember much, we went to my grandmother's house in Bedford for Christmas and Boxing Day, but from the mid-1950s we stayed at home and she came to Cambridge. Our Christmas tree lived in the garden and would be dug up every year and brought in for its few weeks of glory. We always put it just inside the veranda doors in the dining room, to minimise the distance it was carried into the house. All our decorations were homemade and many hours were spent with tinsel, sparkle dust, tin foil and glue. My mother created arrangements of dried flowers, pine cones and teasels painted gold, and even knitted a few fluffy Father Christmases to hang on the tree. Paper chains were hung in every room except the kitchen and bathroom, but including the bedrooms, although my father complained about holes in the walls and picture rails made by the drawing pins. My parents were great writers and receivers of Christmas cards, and these were strung up on loops of string in the lounge. In the escalating excitement of the days before Christmas, there were presents to be wrapped (always with paper recycled from last year) and labels to be made, and the cake to be iced and decorated. The silver three-penny bits had to be retrieved from their little tin in the larder, wrapped in baking parchment and buried in the Christmas pudding.

Like most other fortunate small children, we had stockings in our bedrooms, miraculously filled while we were asleep. I knew it was my father, although I never actually saw him, but I didn't have a chimney or fireplace in my bedroom, so the Santa Claus story always seemed unlikely. The stocking, one of my mother's brown nylons, always had an orange or grapefruit at the bottom but otherwise usually contained 'useful' presents such as crayons and drawing books to colour in, anything to keep us amused for a couple of hours before my parents wanted to get up.

The morning was spent preparing the Christmas dinner which we ate at midday. My mother and grandmother would squabble away in the kitchen about what to put in the stuffing, how often to baste the turkey, or whether to include onion in the white sauce. A great fug would build up in the house, and all the steamed-up windows would pour with condensation. My father would get out the decanter of sherry.

In the afternoon, with very full stomachs, we always went to King's College Chapel for the three o'clock service which was an abbreviated re-run of the broadcast 'Christmas Eve Nine Lessons and Carols'. The joy, of course, was the singing and the purity of the choristers' voices.

Afterwards the adults would debate whether this year's choir and the chorister who'd sung the solo opening verse of 'Once in Royal David's City' were as good as last year's, or whether the choice of carols was appropriate. My father always liked it when they sang 'In the Bleak Midwinter' because the music was written by Harold Darke, who had stood in for Boris Ord at King's in 1941 and whose daughter Olive still lived in Cambridge and came to our church. 'Think of the royalty', he would say, which I imagined to be something to do with the queen. Instead of using the Backs, we had to go in and out of King's from the King's Parade entrance. The colleges closed their gates to the public for at least one day each year to stop them becoming public rights of way, and most chose Christmas Day.

Back at home the cake would be admired and cut, and in the evening my grandmother would sing and strum at the piano or we would play games.

Christmas Day dinner, 1961. (Author's Collection)

On Boxing Day my mother's sister and family usually came over from Bedford for lunch and tea. Barbara and her husband Sidney were chain smokers and the steamy fug of Christmas day was replaced with a different and less pleasant miasma. My uncle John would sometimes visit from London, armed with some strong cider and accompanied by his unruly dog, Mac, who always had to be left in the car and was not allowed into the house. While the adults talked and smoked, my brother and I were expected to play with our cousins. Every year my grandmother would tell us how, when she was a girl, they would follow the Boxing Day hunt which would meet in one of the villages outside Bedford. I don't think that my parents were hunting enthusiasts, or had any friends or acquaintances in the 'country set'. In any event the smallholdings, market gardens and arable farms of north Cambridgeshire were not exactly conducive to foxes or hounds. It was never presented as an option.

Twelfth Night was assiduously observed. The decorations were taken down in the evening, the Christmas tree went back to its spot at the bottom of the garden and everything was put away into the oak trunk with its heavy creaking lid which sat under the window in the lounge, there to stay until the next December.

## THE BIG FREEZE

The perceived wisdom is that Cambridge is a cold and windy place in winter. One imagined in the 1950s shivering students in their draughty rooms, huddled in front of single-bar electric heaters or primitive gas fires. People would remark that Cambridge was exposed to the chilly Arctic winds from the north, and that due east from the Gog Magog Hills there was no higher ground until you reach the Urals in Russia, and therefore no barrier to the icy Siberian blast. For all that, Cambridge is also a dry place, one of the driest in Britain, and rarely receives heavy or prolonged snow.

I never recall a truly white Christmas in Cambridge but the winter of 1962-63 made up for that. There had been chilly easterly winds before Christmas, not unusual for Cambridge, but the temperatures began to fall dramatically between Christmas and New Year and there was a dusting of snow. Hard morning frosts, which again were not uncommon, began to stay for the whole day on the grass. The biting winds had abated and were now replaced by freezing fog in the mornings which left a thick white rime on every branch and twig of every tree and shrub. Even when the sun broke through to reveal a photogenic fairyland, the hoar frost did not melt. On 29 December we went out to Reach Lode and skated on the ice.

There was an established practice in the Fens of benevolent or enthusiastic farmers allowing certain fields to be flooded to a shallow depth in the winter so that even a modest frost would provide some ice. This was particularly true of the meadows or flood plain, known as The Wash, which ran between the Old and New Bedford Rivers north of Earith. This grassland was meant to flood, and was therefore never ploughed, and was unfenced within the high banks of the rivers.

My mother was a keen and expert ice skater and took any opportunity to exploit a fresh layer of ice. With my father's inside knowledge of what conditions were like with water levels, we would usually go to Mepal or Sutton Gault where roads crossed The Wash and there was easy access to the ice. Here my brother and I were taught to skate, on what was probably the largest and safest natural rink in the country, stretching seventeen miles from Earith to Denver sluice, and up to half a mile wide between the banks. Here there was ample room for beginners, village lads playing impromptu games of hockey, gnarled old 'fen tigers' nonchalantly gliding along with their hands clasped behind their backs, and speed skaters racing with giant strides and swinging arms.

In Cambridge the river is effectively a series of sluggish lakes between the weirs and locks and a thin skin of ice was quite a regular occurrence in winter. We would throw small stones or gravel onto the ice to see whether they made a hole or bounced. But soon this skin stretched from bank to bank, forcing the ducks and swans permanently on to land, and began

Garret Hostel Bridge, 19 January 1963. (Author's Collection)

*Above:* Reach Lode on 29 December 1962. (Author's Collection)

*Right:* Getting our skates on, 19 January 1963. (Author's Collection)

to thicken. By the second week of January the first brave souls, mainly dare-devil students, were venturing forth, and their pictures appeared in the evening paper. We soon followed suit, taking our skates down to the frosty grass banks at King's and setting off along the Backs. By the next weekend the whole world seemed to be there, including lots of townspeople who'd never been on the river before, even in a boat, all keen to experience the strange sensation of walking under the bridges. Some people even started cycling along the river from Jesus Green to Silver Street.

In school playgrounds long strips of ice were made by pouring water on the flat tarmac to make skid pans which you would run onto and slide along. The lack of serious hills in Cambridge meant that few people bothered having sledges. We did once take tin trays to the castle mound, but skating was more fun.

In February it snowed heavily and the ice on the river became very rutted, difficult for skating or cycling. The novelty too had worn off, replaced by increased grumbling among the adults about heating bills, frozen pipes and cisterns, and cars and buses which wouldn't start.

Eventually, in early March, it all finished as the temperatures suddenly rose by ten degrees, and the frost, snow and ice melted away as if it had never been there. Even the haggard-looking snowman who had been a fixture on our front lawn for two months, much patched and repaired, dissolved into a small grey pile of sludge. The mufflers, woolly hats and skates were packed away for another year, but there never was another year like 1963. Unless something funny happens to the Gulf Stream, there probably never will be.

## GARDENING

My parents were avid gardeners. My mother had trained and worked as a florist at Moyse Stevens in Berkeley Square before she was married and had unusual horticultural knowledge. She seemed to know the name of every flower and every plant. My father knew little but was a willing and strong worker. I and my brother were intermittently willing workers.

Our back garden was long and thin, about 25ft wide but over 200 feet long and divided for most of its length by a central path of concrete slabs. On the south side, next to our neighbours, was grass with two tall pear trees and five old apple trees, all of which pre-dated the house and were once part of a commercial orchard. North of the path, between that and the hedge to Roseford Road, was the vegetable patch, and at the bottom of the garden, the compost heap, raspberry canes, gooseberry bushes and two big Bramley apple trees.

This potentially utilitarian layout was relieved by a rose pergola near the house, and several small flower beds beside the path which spawned hollyhocks.

My parents grew all the usual things – potatoes, runner beans, peas, carrots, beetroot and cabbage, and radishes and lettuces under cloches – but we also had asparagus, courgettes, rhubarb and strawberries which were slightly more exotic in the austere post-war years. The seasonal cycles of digging, hoeing, sowing, weeding, and picking were soon engrained in my calendar. Seeing the first heads poking through the sandy ridge of the asparagus bed, or the rhubarb thrusting up through the straw which had been packed into the open-topped metal buckets were events to be savoured, among the more mundane chores of picking up fallen apples, hedge clippings or gathering up the little piles of weeds collected by my mother. Sweeping up leaves in the autumn with the besom and rake seemed a never-ending task.

Picking the apples and pears was a precarious and communal task, with ladders extended to their maximum range to reach the best and ripest at the top of the pear trees. Even with the long picker

The fascination of bonfires, 5 November 1960. (Author's collection)

and its net on the end of the pole, one or two of the pears were elusive. Standing on the top of the rickety wooden stepladder to reach the biggest apples required nerve and balance, and someone below to stop it wobbling. My mother would fastidiously sort the fruit, looking for maggots and blemishes, and wrap the good ones in newspaper to be stored in the wooden pallets which were stacked in the shed. Some of the eating apples lasted almost until the next year's harvest.

The raspberries and strawberries involved a constant battle with the birds. We used to put nets over the plants in which the blackbirds and thrushes often got entangled, and then had to be set free, with admonishing words from my mother.

I liked helping most with bonfires, particularly if there were lots of flames, not just billows of smoke from damp vegetation. In the winter when it was dark, early I would look out from my bedroom window to see if the bonfire was still going, or first thing on a Sunday morning run down to see if there were still any hot embers from Saturday's blaze.

The front garden was much more for public display, and my mother's chief pride and joy, with a multitude of bulbs, annuals and perennials in the herbaceous border. At the front was a laburnum tree, with its vivid yellow flowers and intriguing seed pods which were inevitably fascinating when told how poisonous they were. There was a yew and sumac tree against the fence with Roseford Road and a young holly which for a few years grew at exactly the same rate as my brother. Beside the front corner of the house was a giant flowering currant bush whose fragrance seemed to fill the whole month of April. My mother also nurtured a little rockery, with cacti and succulents, which over the years became a receptacle for numerous geological trophies from our holidays. It might puzzle some future archaeologist.

In the summer there were always vases of flowers in the house, and in the winter strong-scented hyacinths grew in pots on every windowsill. My mother was in charge of doing the floral arrangements in church, which included buying flowers or asking others to provide them from their own gardens, as we also did. Having Dear's Nursery directly opposite our house was a boon. Whenever we were out in the country she was always on the lookout for bulrushes, catkins or teasels, or anything else that might be useful. Bunches of dried Japanese lanterns and asters, tied with twine, hung from the wooden rafters of the garage and garden shed.

My mother loved visiting other gardens when they were open to the public, which I as a child considered a great drudgery. While I liked visiting the University Botanical Gardens for their big cedar trees, the lake, the bamboo groves and what looked like monstrous prickly rhubarb, I didn't appreciate my mother's concern for the Latin names of plants. I shared my father's disinterest in the nomenclature of flowers and shrubs, although it is extraordinary how much later in life one remembers of things one never sought to remember.

## A PLAIN DIET

Much of what we ate was related to the garden and what it produced. We were therefore used to the intermittent gluts of various fruits and vegetables during the summer and autumn. For me some of these deluges, such as the glorious couple of weeks of asparagus in early May or the raspberries in August, didn't last long enough, whereas the runner beans, the rhubarb and the cabbage seemed to go on and on forever. I should, however, remain grateful to have had the good fortune as a child to enjoy the immediacy and fresh taste of peas picked, podded and cooked, or new potatoes excavated, washed of their soil, boiled and eaten within half an hour.

My mother had dozens of glass Kilner jars with glass stoppers and metal clamps which were put to constant use to deal with surplus produce. The salting and bottling of runner beans seemed a continuous process in the summer, so much so that I suspected that in the enthusiasm for preserving these tough stringy objects, the opportunity of eating them in a more appealing, younger and more tender state was lost. The result was a grey-mauve sludge which we had to endure throughout the year.

Plums, greengages, gooseberries and blackcurrants were also bottled, while strawberries, raspberries and apples, sometimes with blackberries thrown in, were made into jam or jelly. My mother used a huge aluminium preserving pan which she also used for making marmalade

The back garden in springtime, 1967. (Author's Collection)

when the Seville oranges were available in December. Normally the pan hung on a hook in the outside lavatory, and when I was small it improvised as a modest outdoor paddling pool in the garden. It certainly held a lot of jam.

We had no refrigerator, and although the pantry faced north and had a stone floor, summer heat waves were a problem. On those stiflingly hot July and August days when the garden was full of flying ants and the pavements smelt of melting tar, we put the milk into bowls of water with wet tea towels or muslin cloths draped over the bottles acting as a wick; 'latent heat of evaporation', so my father explained. It worked tolerably well but sometimes the milk would curdle, and then my mother would make scones so as not to waste anything.

The dreaded ordeal at infant school of being made to drink a third of a pint of milk at morning break-time, when the crates had been left standing in the full glare of the sun, very quickly gave me a strong aversion, approaching nausea, to warm frothing milk. I yearned for winter mornings when the milk on the doorstep or in the playground was icy cold, when the breakfast cereal remained crunchy in the bowl and when the school-time milk could be quaffed without any sensation of taste.

Our diet was simple to the point of plainness. My mother's culinary ambitions were limited, very much in the Mrs Beaton school of traditional pre-war English cooking. Elizabeth David or Robert Carrier were unheard of. Besides, my father didn't like onions, garlic or tomatoes, or thought they didn't agree with him, and also disliked any form of pasta or rice. My mother certainly did all the cooking, and while my father would help with the washing up, and make my brother and I do the drying, he probably hardly knew how to boil an egg. Neither of my parents liked anything spicy. Six years in India had put them off the very smell of curry, let alone the taste of anything exotic.

Sunday lunch was the main meal of the week, with a joint of meat, roast potatoes and vegetables, with maybe a treacle pudding, stewed or baked apples to follow, always with Birds custard, which I loathed, especially the skin. In the early 1960s my mother discovered Angel Delight, which was some sort of powder which when mixed with milk turned into a lurid sweet confection. There was a similar packet for making lemon meringue pies.

Leftovers were always kept for re-use, placed in little bowls on the pantry shelves. The remains of the Sunday joint would be minced and incorporated into a shepherd's pie together with leftover carrots or peas. Potatoes would be mashed and reheated. Otherwise, during the week the evening meal, or 'high tea' as we called it, eaten at six o'clock, would comprise a fry-up of egg, sausage or fish fingers, followed by bread and butter and a piece of homemade cake.

As a toddler I liked to help my mother mix the ingredients for cakes, mainly so that I could lick the bowl. Even what turned out to be the dullest sponge was scrumptious uncooked. I even preferred it to the icing which too fast turned to cement in the mixing bowl. Similarly my mother's pastry, made with lard and hard white flour, which was like concrete when baked, was delicious in its raw state.

For fruit we had our apples, carefully stored and eked out to last almost the whole year, and a glut of pears in the autumn. We bought bananas from Mr Wiseman, and sometimes grapefruit. Oranges, tangerines and mandarins were a treat, usually only around Christmas time. The enormous range of imported tropical fruit which fill our shops today – kiwi fruit, mangos, pomegranates, lychees, cranberries and cumquats – were simply not on sale then, and even if they had, would have been beyond the pocket of my parents.

In provincial Cambridge in the 1950s and '60s, today's commonplace products such as humous, taramasalata, marinated olives, chorizo, prosciutto or parmesan were all scarcely heard of. Sainsbury's sold lots of bacon and English ham, but otherwise cold meats were limited to hazlet, corned beef from Argentina, luncheon meat or spam.

My parents drank tea for breakfast, after lunch, and at high tea, and my father being a northerner liked it strong and stewed. Exotic or herbal teas, such as Earl Grey, Lapsang or camomile were unknown. Hardly anyone, it seemed, drank real coffee, and my mother only ever offered it in percolated form to guests at the end of an evening. For a while she used a bottle of Camp coffee essence (mainly full of chicory) which was probably acceptable in coffee cake icing, but disgusting as a drink. Later she bought small amounts of beans roasted on the counter in Matthews or Sainsbury's. I hated tea and when as a teenager I insisted on having coffee, it was Nescafé instant.

Generally my brother and I were given very diluted orange squash to drink. Despite its undoubted chemical composition, it tasted vaguely of oranges, but we never had real orange juice to make a comparison. Fizzy drinks were a special treat, only ever provided by a visitor or Mrs Maskell, and my parents distinctly frowned on the very idea of coca cola. I did once have a bottle of Lucozade when I was ill. Otherwise invalid food comprised warm bread and milk or Bovril, both of which were excellent incentives to get better.

Probably the unhealthiest part of our diet was the amount of frying and eggs. My mother always gave us a cooked breakfast, eggs fried in lard with fried bread and a rasher of bacon. Then we had fried eggs again for tea, perhaps, as a treat, broken over a portion of chips bought from the fish and chip shop in Histon Road, the liquid yoke mingling with the flaccid fatty potatoes. The only respite was boiled eggs on Sundays. No wonder my father began to put on weight when he reached his forties, and had a heart attack in his fifties. I don't think that cholesterol was part of the vocabulary then.

We never ate out, unless invited to do so by friends or relations more affluent than us. Indeed the number of restaurants in Cambridge in the '50s and '60s was very limited, and 'foreign' places such as the Taj Mahal on Regent Street, the Gardenia in Rose Crescent or the Hang Chow off Petty Cury were strictly off limits for my parents. The Civic in Petty Cury (more formally the Cambridge Borough Restaurant) was considered dowdy by my mother. Anything smarter was prohibitively expensive. The best was reckoned to be the Pink Geranium in Melbourn, but I never went there. Pubs hadn't started doing food, apart from pickled onions and packets of crisps, not that my parents ever went to pubs. Gastropubs were still decades away. Students ate in college dining rooms, and even greasy spoon cafes were few and far between.

Even on holiday we rarely ate out. The norm would be a picnic lunch and then some sort of 'meat-and two-veg' cooked meal in our guest house. My mother firmly resisted camping or caravanning, quite understandably wanting a rest from the daily chores of kitchen stove and sink.

From today's perspective all this seems austere and dull, but it was, quite simply, what everybody did. How the nation's habits have changed.

## TRANSPORT

A major perk of my father's job was that he was provided with a car. I don't believe he got much choice in what it was, but it came with free insurance and free servicing at Marshall's or in the work's depot. All we had to pay for was petrol for private use, the mileage of which my father carefully wrote down in a little book kept under the dashboard.

At that time car ownership was low, and cars were far more expensive relative to income than today. We were lucky although I didn't realise it at the time; I took it for granted that cars were an integral part of life. This was mainly because of my grandmother's long and almost pioneering association with motor vehicles and her penchant for talking about it. As a tomboy teenager in a prosperous shop-keeping family in Bedford around the turn of the century, she had been one of the first women to ride a motorbike. After the First World War, when her husband disappeared and left her as a single parent with three young children, she became a bus driver to earn a living, not a normal profession for a woman. In 1948 when aged sixty she had to retire from the buses, and she started her own driving school. This was rather grandly called 'The Wings School of Motoring', although it was just her, and with her split-screen Morris Minor, she became a familiar part of Bedford life. Quite remarkably, the indomitable Mrs Gooch continued to teach and get people through their test well into her eighties, even though by then she had replaced her split-screen Morris for a single-screen version. She was also knowledgeable about engines and gear boxes, and did most of the routine servicing on her car, always a ready topic of conversation with my father. Road improvement schemes, new bypasses, the new M1 motorway, and the plans and policies of Ernest Marples were constantly discussed, alongside the complaints about extra and heavier lorries on the roads.

Our first car that I can remember was a Vauxhall Wyvern, which was the customary black and had red leather seats, and so too was the grander Vauxhall Velox which followed it. My mother was full of praise for the size of the boot in the Velux, particularly when we went on holiday. By good fortune my father was able to change the work car every three years, and in 1961 traded the Velux for a new Vauxhall Victor FB, with its racy curves and streamlined bonnet. It was pale blue, not black, and altogether seemed jazzier and more modern, and an appropriate colour for Cambridge. My mother, though, was disappointed that the boot was smaller, so we got a roof rack as a supplement.

After that we had an Austin Cambridge, in a pale cream hue, and then an Austin 1800 which I considered squat and ugly. For a short while in the late 1960s we were a two-car family, when we bought a little second-hand red mini, the height of current fashion, mainly for my brother to get to work in Stanmore in his gap year.

Traffic and parking in Cambridge was always a great talking-point among my parents, friends and relatives, although as a child I found such conversation or diatribe tedious. However, sitting in traffic jams on Victoria Road as through traffic from Huntingdon Road and the north struggled to get round Mitchams Corner and over the bridge to Victoria Avenue, Newmarket Road and the east was equally tiresome. Queens' Road, or 'the Backs', Fen Causeway, Lensfield Road and Parker's Piece also endured heavy lorry traffic trying to navigate a way through Cambridge, belching out their sickly diesel fumes en route.

Train spotting with John Sharpe, 1963. (Author's Collection)

I and probably my parents too were unaware of the Holford-Wright Report of 1950 which proposed new road building in Cambridge to relieve the pressure. Such documents in those days were not much publicised, let alone subject to public consultation. Little did I know too that later in life I would share a house in London with Myles Wright's daughter, Hannah.

Until 1890 there had been only one public road bridge over the River Cam in the town, the Great Bridge beside Magdalene College. The Cam Bridges Act of 1889 allowed two more to be built, and one of these was Victoria Bridge, opened in 1890, with Victoria Avenue driven across Midsummer Common, the other being Fen Causeway. Mitcham's Corner remained a bottleneck, even with the roundabout built in 1967. The route for another bridge was proposed in 1950 but not carried out until 1970 when the new Elizabeth Way bridge at last provided a new relief road from Milton Road to Newmarket Road, connecting too with East Road, Parkside and Lensfield Road. At the opening ceremony in July 1971, Lord (Rab) Butler, then high Steward of Cambridge, struggled to cut the ribbon with the pair of golden scissors which he'd been given. Despite all that, pressure was relieved from north and east Cambridge.

Fortunately various other Holford-Wright proposals were never implemented. The so-called 'northern relief road' would have driven a new road from the Huntingdon Road-Histon Road junction, running east of the castle mound and County Hall, over a new bridge, across Jesus Green, through Jesus College, to link with Jesus Lane. Of this crazy plan only the Park Street multi-storey car park was built, in 1963, one of the ugliest buildings in Cambridge. They even proposed that Mill Lane become a main road with a new bridge across the Mill Pond, to bypass the narrow bit of Silver Street. Instead in 1959 the Silver Street bridge was widened and rebuilt, to the pre-war designs of Edwin Lutyens.

The ongoing problem of through-traffic, and particularly the ever-increasing size of trucks and articulated lorries, was only solved with the bypasses. Holford and Wright had proposed these in 1950 but it took another twenty-five years for fruition. The decline of the London docks and the massive growth of Felixstowe as a container port in the 1970s, helped by a non-unionised workforce, caused an explosion in lorry movements form the industrial Midlands to Ipswich on the old A45 Bedford to Newmarket route. The Northern bypass became top priority, and was opened in 1978. The problem of west Cambridge was more thorny, and there were endless debates in the 1950s and '60s about possible roads across Grantchester meadows, Byron's Pool, the Coton footpath and the American cemetery at Madingley. Eventually there was a big public inquiry in 1973, lasting six months, to decide the route. The construction of the M11 from London to Stump Cross between 1972 and 1977 eventually provided a solution for the west and the south. From Stump Cross the Western bypass was built to join the Huntingdon Road beyond Girton, keeping well clear of Grantchester and sunk into a cutting for long stretches, although culminating in an intersection which devoured lots of land without providing all the necessary connections. A Southern bypass wasn't deemed to be needed.

It is hard today to imagine a Cambridge without the bypasses. On the other hand perhaps it wasn't that bad before. This also was a time before road closures, width restrictions, speed humps, rising bollards, yellow lines and parking meters, and all the other paraphernalia of traffic management. There were only a few one-way streets in the centre of Cambridge, just Petty Cury and the anti-clockwise triangle of Trinity Street, Market Street and Sidney Street. There were just a handful of traffic lights, at the bottom of Castle and at the junction of Hills Road and Lensfield Road by the Catholic Church. The only pedestrian crossings were zebras, with their orange flashing Belisha beacons, and newly introduced 'lollypop' ladies. Ideas of park-and-ride, road pricing or other such constraints hadn't been dreamt of.

My father always drove to his office in Brooklands Avenue, usually came home for a cooked lunch and returned to the office presumably almost within an hour. He can't have spent too much time in traffic jams. Two or three times a week he would have to go out into the Fens to inspect various drainage works or pumping stations. As for the rest of us, we used our bikes.

Learning to ride a bicycle was high on the agenda. As a toddler my mother put me on a little seat mounted immediately behind the front handle bars and capacious wicker basket of her sturdy Humber and would venture off with me down to the town centre and take me to Infant School in Milton Road. From this advanced and elevated position there was a good view and a chance to learn some road sense. It wasn't long before I progressed from my cherished red tricycle to a two-wheeler, initially with my energetic father running along with me on the pavement holding the saddle, but then one spring afternoon on the back garden lawn, I experienced the unnerving thrill of the hand no longer being there. The little red tricycle sat in the back of the shed for a few years, but was then given away. Sadly there was to be no Citizen Kane 'rosebud' for me.

Everybody in Cambridge seemed to ride a bike and despite the amount of traffic it was not seen as particularly dangerous. Perhaps there was a 'safety in numbers' attitude. When I started at the Perse Preparatory Junior School, over three miles away in Trumpington Road, my father or our neighbour Harry Smith took me by car in the morning and I would come home by bus. But by the time I was eleven and starting at the County High School in Hills Road, I was cycling.

The volume of cycling in Cambridge was unusual. In the summer of 1968 a survey was carried out at the County Boys' school of how pupils travelled; 35 per cent came by bike, 50 per cent by bus, 10 per cent on foot and only 5 per cent by car. That is remarkable given that half the pupils came from outlying villages, not from the city. I doubt whether those figures are the same today, when, despite the best endeavours of Sustrans, the national average for cycling to school is only 2 per cent. It didn't really cross our minds that cycling was dangerous until one dark, rainy December evening in 1962, Peter Lapwood, who was the undergraduate son of Ralph and Nancy Lapwood at church, was killed cycling on the Babraham road. After that there was extra vigilance about carrying bicycle lights at night, big, heavy and battery-hungry though they were.

There were two rival bus companies in Cambridge: Eastern Counties which were red and Premier Travel which were blue. Both had double-deckers, and open platforms at the back, just like the old London buses. My journey home meant changing buses at Drummer Street, which was a dump then and not a pleasant place to hang around. To get away from the gangs of older children, I used to walk up and down the new Bradwell Court arcade which had been opened in 1960. The bus to Histon was usually packed with older boys going out to the more distant villages of Cottenham, Rampton or Willingham. Sometimes the bullies among them would kidnap school caps or satchels and only release them or throw them out of a window when the victim's stop had long been passed. I quickly learnt, having once had to walk back from Histon village green, to avoid sitting upstairs and to keep within sight of the conductor on the lower deck.

As a family group I don't think we ever travelled by train, except when we were on holiday in Scotland and took a day trip on the Highland line from Craigendoran. In Cambridge the car was cheaper, and we were miles from the station. My first experience of trains was the level crossing at Histon, close to Chivers Jam factory. Here a man in a greasy peaked cap would open and close the big wooden gates which came across the road, and then retreat to the signal box. This branch line to St Ives carried passenger and freight trains throughout the 1950s, until it was closed through 'lack of demand' and became abandoned and overgrown.

For a few crazy years, from about eleven to thirteen, I became a fanatical train spotter, encouraged by a school comrade John Sharpe. He lived in Claremont, very near the station, and he and his father knew everything there was to know about steam trains and the new diesels. Hundreds of hours were spent leaning on the fence of the cattle market beside the tracks between the Hills Road bridge and the end of the station platforms, taking down numbers and crossing them off later at home in the little books which printed lists of all the numbers. The excitement when engineering works at Huntingdon diverted the East Coast mainline services through Cambridge knew no bounds.

Once I went on my own by train to Bedford on the line which ran through Gamlingay and Sandy, and passed Manor Farm in Toft where my school friend John Tebbit lived. A lot of people said how sad it was when this line closed in 1964, although the new space-age telescopes at Lord's Bridge seemed like progress at the time, taking advantage of the precisely east-west tracks. It is ironic and satisfying now that the St Ives line will live again as a new guided bus or tram route.

My brother and I were very keen to learn to drive. When we were quite young we would sometimes sit on my father's lap while he drove along a quiet fenland road and practice steering. When our legs were long enough he took us out to the disused aerodrome at Bourn. Here on the wide expanses of wartime concrete runways (now vanishing under the noddy-boxes of Cambourn) we could learn the co-ordination skills of changing gears and three-point turns without endangering anyone else.

Both my parents had got their driving licenses before the war when there was no requirement to take a test, and my grandmother was critical of their bad habits. As a back-seat observer, I was always nervous of my father's overtaking when he would lean forward and bite his lower lip as if to urge the car to greater speed. I particularly disliked three-lane roads where the central lane was a form of Russian roulette.

When it came to learning 'properly' it was inevitable that I was subjected to my grandmother's strict regime of hand-brake starts, speed control and emergency stops. Her Morris Minor had indicator flaps called 'trafficators' on each side, rather than flashing tail lights, and hand signals had to be perfected for every manoeuvre.

I took my test at the earliest opportunity and had a most benevolent examiner. Starting off from outside the office in Station Road we did a minimal circuit of left turns around Tenison Road, Glisson Road and Hills Road. I read, correctly, a number plate on a nearby car and told him what colour followed green in the order of traffic lights. It was all over in ten minutes. Perhaps he was desperate for his lunch. My grandmother had always said that Cambridge was a good place to take your test, and on that showing, she was right.

## EXCURSIONS

Supposedly nowhere in Britain is more than seventy-two miles from the sea, but Cambridge must be quite close to wherever that is. The nearest coast was a long drive through the slow wiggly roads of Suffolk, Norfolk or Essex, and hardly worth a day trip. We did, once or twice, go to Brancaster, near Cromer, where the tide receded about three miles across an enormous flat expanse of sand, and raced in again at alarming speed. During the Easter holidays my grandmother, in her Morris Minor, would go for a week to stay in Clacton-on-Sea, usually in the Waverley guest house or if she was feeling flush and accompanied by her two wealthy elderly friends, Dorie and May, then in the Esplanade Hotel on Marine Parade.

Because my brother was the oldest grandchild, he had the dubious privilege of going too and the rest of us would drive over to Clacton at the end of the week to bring him back. Apart from the beach, with its timber groins and freezing North Sea water, and the pier, there seemed little to commend Clacton, certainly not for a week. The promenade with its lurid floral displays, hooped railings, bandstands and benches seemed stultifyingly ordered.

Brancaster, 1960. (Author's Collection)

My brother's scout group went for summer camps to Holkham Hall on the north Norfolk coast, which similarly we visited at the end of the week. The parkland with its flat-bottomed trees looked much the same to me as Wimpole Hall, and I wondered why they bothered to go so far. Wimpole at that time was lived in by the reclusive Elsie Bambridge, daughter of Rudyard Kipling, and no doubt less inclined to allow visitors or campers than the benevolent Earl of Leicester at Holkham.

Trips to Bedford to see my grandmother, aunts and uncles were so frequent that they didn't count as 'special', when all we did was visit their houses. Occasionally we went on an excursion from Bedford, which invariably involved a picnic. My grandmother was fond in spring of a place called Brown's Wood which was near Odell Great Wood, ten miles north of Bedford. There was a disused wartime aerodrome nearby, still with hangers and concrete runways, but the woods were full of bluebells and primroses, and pinky-white flowers which she called milk maids but which were probably wood anemones. Sometimes we went to Woburn Sands at Aspley Guise or the woods at Clophill, south of Bedford, where the hills seemed dramatically steep compared to anything around Cambridge. Here we would roam along grassy tracks beneath the pines collecting cones, watching out for deer in the distance and ant hills in the sandy banks. There was talk amongst the adults of James Hanratty and the A6 murders, which I found disconcerting.

Closer to home, but still relying on the car, were trips to Royston Heath, Newmarket Heath and Wandlebury. What we called Royston Heath is properly named Therfield Heath, part of the chalk scarp which runs across south Cambridgeshire. Here there were mature beech woods to explore, the ground crunching with fallen nuts and last autumn's leaves, the trunks tall and smooth and wide enough to hide behind. The golf-course in front of the woods provided smooth greens for my brother to fly and land his model planes and gliders. Sometimes we found abandoned golf balls in the brambles or long grass. Once, being careful not to be seen, we moved a wayward ball to within an inch of the hole, much to the amazement of the player and disbelief of his opponent.

At Newmarket we went to the hills and woods near Gazeley, again part of the chalk ridge. This was the best place we knew to fly a kite, as the rising grounds caught and magnified every

Woburn Sands, with grandmother, 1960. (Author's Collection)

breath of wind. Below us were the stud farms and fenced-off rides for the racehorse stables, and the long narrow lines of pine trees which distinguish this part of the county. On the way home we would pass the gypsy grave at the crossroads, always carefully adorned with fresh flowers. We once stopped to read the inscription to 'Joseph, the Unknown Gypsy Boy'.

My mother's aversion to gypsies and tinkers meant that my brother and I were kept well away from the great Midsummer Fair, held every June on Midsummer Common. This was a direct successor to the ancient Stourbridge Fair, once one of Europe's largest trading fairs, but this historical pedigree cut no ice with my mother. Midsummer Fair was exclusively a funfair, run mainly by the Thurston family of nomadic showmen, and was considered by my mother to be a place to lose well-earned money, or worse, to be pick-pocketed. Candy floss, helter-skelters, big wheels, walls-of-death and ghost trains were, sadly, not part of my childhood. We did once go to Billy Smart's Circus, and saw the clowns, lion-tamers, sea lions and palamino ponies. As with the fair, the churned-up grass took weeks to recover.

Once a year, always in May when the azaleas were out, my parents had their own excursion, leaving my brother and I at home. This was a 'works' outing, funded by Gwynnes Pumps, who laid on a weekend for selected clients and their wives at the Woodhall Spa hotel in Lincolnshire. My father and his colleagues at the Great Ouse River Board were good customers for their pumps and engines. My mother and father loved the glamour of the occasion, a rare chance to relive the atmosphere of their pre-1947 colonial days in India. Usually our grandmother came over from Bedford to mind the fort, and spoil us with fizzy lemonade or ginger beer.

The closest friends my parents had made in India were David and Eileen Rogers. David worked for the Foreign Office and shared my father's passion for rugby and cricket. Several times we visited their dreary suburban house in Walton-on-Thames before going to the Middlesex Sevens at Twickenham. The Gillette Factory and construction works for the Chiswick flyover left just as big an impression, much praised by my parents after the queues on the then unimproved North Circular and Hanger Lane.

The most exciting trips were to London to visit my father's elder brother, John. We either went on the slow old road through Ware, Broxbourne and Hoddesdon, or turned off at Royston to join the A1 at Baldock. The Great North Road had the excitement of bypasses and dual carriageways, the Comet at Hatfield, and the line of Lombardy poplars near South Mimms which my mother had remembered being planted before the war, and into one of which poor Dennis Brain crashed. The first sighting of a Green Line bus was a sure sign of the approaching capital. London had bigger buildings and wider streets than anything in Cambridge and seemed a place of unimaginable size and unfathomable mystery. It also had trolley buses and neon advertisements, and the strange subterranean world which was the Tube. John lived in Ainger Road which was, and still is, a quiet street between Primrose Hill and Chalk Farm. At the bottom of the road beyond the shabby shops on Regent's Park Road was the arched-girder bridge over the cutting of the Euston railway where we loved to stand and be engulfed by steam as a train passed beneath. At the top of the road was the park with its paths leading up to the summit from where London lay spread out below.

John lived in a maisonette at the top of a five-storey house in a grimy grey brick terrace. Shadowy people who we never really saw lived on the basement, ground and first floors and we had to pass their doors as we climbed up the many flights of stairs. On the first half-landing everyone had to share the single lavatory, which had a huge mahogany seat, cold blue lino on the floor and 'tracing paper' type loo roll..

John was an actor and a bachelor although he shared his flat with an Australian journalist Ernest. Every surface was covered with books and scripts, music scores and librettos, newspaper cuttings and reviews, and the whole flat smelt of a curious mixture of dog and snuff. In the kitchen stood a rickety and probably rather dangerous gas stove, and a badly stained bath which was usually piled high with unwashed cups, mugs and plates. My mother thought the place a tip and never gave up hinting that John should tidy up. To me it was enchanting, bohemian, adventurous, artistic, the opposite of home.

Ainger Road was our base from which we would venture forth into the metropolis, to the Science or Natural History Museums, the Plantetarium, a trip on the river to Greenwich, Lord's Cricket Ground or a Kenwood lakeside concert. Occasionally we went to a West End theatre, once to see John who was playing alongside Bernard Miles in *Treasure Island* at the Duke of York. My parents keenly followed John's career, listened to every broadcast of 'Doctor Finlay's Casebook' in which he appeared and scoured *The Telegraph* for reviews of anything he was in. He had taken the stage name Dunbar, although we never knew why, other than it sounded Scottish and he specialised in Scots accents.

John loved Hampstead Heath and often we would drive in his shabby mini-van to the Vale of Health or Well Walk and set off into the woods and meadows. Here his dog Mac could run free and chase all the other dogs, and worry the ducks by jumping into the ponds.

When I was a teenager and had to come up to London for auditions or to go on National Youth Orchestra courses, John would meet me off trains at King's Cross or Liverpool Street. I went with him to Covent Garden where we sat high in the 'gods' of the upper slips to hear *Die Meistersingers*, *The Flying Dutchman*, *Don Carlos* and *Rosenkavalier*. Afterwards we would pick our way outside through the cabbage leaves, squashed oranges and broken crates of the fruit and vegetable market and call into a long thin smoky bar behind the Strand. In the hot fug John would introduce me to some of his thespian friends, and I would try to look older than I was. The Rosslyn Hill Tavern was another of his haunts, serving his favourite tipple, scrumpy from wooden barrels. When I stayed at his flat we would take Mac for a late night run on Primrose Hill and I would gaze at all the lights twinkling in the distance, which seemed like a scene out of *101 Dalmatians*. I slept on the sofa and dreamt of a life in London.

# WANDLEBURY AND THE ROMAN ROAD

North Cambridge is a flat and drab landscape and even the most modest hills in the vicinity to the west and south seemed exciting to young eyes, and later into adolescence took on almost romantic qualities. Of all the little humps and bumps around Cambridge my favourite was Wandlebury Ring, up on the Gog Magog Hills. Daniel Defoe, with a touch of irony, described these chalky hills as 'mountains', but everything of course is relative.

One of our standard Sunday afternoon walks was to park the car in the gravelly lay-by on Worts Causeway, above Limekiln Road, near the thin strip of beech woods, and pick up the beginning of the Roman Road.

The *Via Devana*, as the Romans called it, ran from Colchester to Godmanchester and presumably forded or bridged the Cam near the present Magdalene Bridge. The section north-west of Cambridge is followed and obliterated by the modern A14 road, but south-east of Cambridge, running across the Gog Magog Hills and down to Haverhill, it is an unmade-up bridleway, a straight rutted track flanked by hedges. Although I didn't grumble about walking as much as my brother (indeed I half-believed my father's flattery that I had sturdy legs and was a good walker), I found the Roman Road dull. Through gaps in the hedges of hawthorn and elder there were glimpses of fields of corn, vast expanses of green, fawn or brown, depending on the season, the twittering of skylarks and the alarm calls of the hedgerow birds, but there was little to do except walk. Occasionally we drove out to Babraham and parked on the verge of the main Newmarket Road and walked in the other direction, towards Cambridge. Although I thought little of it at the time, these gently rolling hills, sharply silhouetted against the sky, were etched into the brain and became the bench-mark against which to compare other landscapes in the future, far and wide.

Wandlebury, which the Roman Road skirts, was far more enthralling. I was not the first or last to be entranced by the mysteries of Wandlebury Ring and the legends of Gog and Magog. In the eighteenth century it was recorded that the figure of a giant was cut into the chalk hillside, rather like the Cerne Abbas man in Dorset. In the early 1950s the archaeologist T.C. Lethbridge tried to show that various undulations in the turf indicated the outlines of other mythical figures, such as a three-breasted woman astride a pair of horses, a chariot, and even the figure of the Earth Mother, Magog. He went so far as to publish a book called

The old stables, Wandlebury.

*Gog and Magog: the Buried Gods.* The lumps and hollows were later shown to be natural geological phenomena, not man made or supernatural. In the 1970s there were some who claimed that the site was related to ley lines and the constellations, theories also soon debunked.

Although the estate had been acquired by the Cambridge Preservation Society in 1937 and was open to the public, it was in a neglected and wild state in the 1950s. The big house, built by the Godolphin family in the 1730s, had fallen into rack and ruin and was pulled down in 1956, leaving just the grand stable block with its picturesque clock and cupola.

The ancient earthwork ring runs half a mile around the house and its deep ditch and steep banks were a perfect adventure playground. Huge dark yew trees overhung the sides, while the trunks of fallen beeches, blown over in gales, provided gang planks or bridges to balance on and scramble across. Under the quaint little brick bridge which carried the access driveway to the mansion, the culvert tunnel was a place to hide or generate an echo. At the time I found it hard to believe that this had been an Iron Age fort, built to repel the invading Iceni tribe. Wandlebury was so thickly wooded and overgrown that it was hard to imagine how, even if it was on a hill-top, it could have commanded views across the surrounding countryside. Instead I imagined enemy warriors creeping up through the undergrowth, undetected, and over-running the defences.

Not many other people went to Wandlebury, and it certainly had not by then been sanitised into a country park, with sign-posted walks and information boards, neat paths and a car park where you pay. Often we seemed to have the place all to ourselves. Best of all was the 'secret garden', reached through a broken wooden door in the high brick walls near the remains of the old house. The walls were smothered in rampant ivy and creepers which made the door hard to find. Inside this 'lost world' were gnarled old apple trees, choked with moss, long grass and chest-high patches of nettles, and in one corner a row of animal graves marked with small stones, perhaps pet dogs or maybe some of the blood-stock horses which were bred from the Godolphin Arabian, Britain's first imported Arab stallion. His burial spot was marked with a tablet in the stables archway.

Birthday party at Wandlebury, 30 June 1962. From left to right: Tiplady, Young, myself, Tebbit, Dawson and Dean. (Author's Collection)

My parents knew that I loved Wandlebury, so it was here at the end of June that I had my birthday picnic for several successive years, sharing the magic and exploration with three or four friends from school. So was formed a rose-tinted memory of perfect summer days and a nostalgia for how Wandlebury used to be.

# CHURCHES AND CHAPELS

Familiarity breeds contempt, and for that reason alone I never found Emmanuel Congregational Church a beautiful or awe-inspiring place. As an architectural critic I was in good company, because Pevsner, in his 1954 edition of *The Buildings of England*, lambasted the prominence of the tower, 'big, extremely harsh, asserting itself much too self-confidently'. The same of course can be said about another of James Cubitt's non-conformist buildings, the Union Chapel in Islington, which also has a colossal and dominating spire, but which is generally more highly regarded.

The inside of Emmanuel is very plain, even more so since 1991 when the old dark pews were removed and the floor re-laid in pale timber. In the apse or sanctuary the stained-glass lancet windows by Morris & Co. appropriately depict puritans with Cambridge connections, notably Oliver Cromwell and John Milton. The functional side extension, also built in 1991 and designed by Bland Brown & Cole, doesn't do much to help the frontage to Trumpington Street in architectural terms. Emmanuel also has no outside space to relieve its bulk. At the rear with a narrow door onto Little St Mary's is the caretaker's flat, but the minister's manse is in Hurst Park Avenue off Milton Road. We occasionally visited, mainly for my mother to raid the garden for flowers and greenery for the church.

The preachers who I remember as a child all had affable and sympathetic qualities, and despite the lack of visual ornament and the simplicity of the services, there was no hint of 'eternal hell and damnation'. John Murray was greatly revered, and all those who came after he left in 1956 were measured by my parents against him. Dick Hall was a benign, down-to-earth, round-faced man who had come from and eventually returned to London where he became Moderator (the Congregational equivalent of a bishop). My mother became very friendly with his wife Gwen, mainly through flower arranging. David Geddes, who followed in 1965, was more cerebral and academic, and although my brother got on rather well for a time with one of the daughters, he seemed rather high and mighty. Tony Coates ,who succeeded Geddes, was younger and more dynamic, and keen on reform, but he moved on in 1982. Derek Wales became a good counsel to my parents in their old age, particularly my mother after my father died.

Emmanuel was twinned with St Columba's Presbyterian Church in Downing Street and occasionally we went there for a combined service. It seemed even more unassuming and gloomier inside than Emmanuel. It formally merged with Emmanuel in 1972. More interesting were the rare collaborations with St Mary-the-Less, or Little St Mary's as we knew it, which was right next door to Emmanuel on Trumpington Street. Sheltered by its big yew trees, tall railings and pretty churchyard, more garden than graveyard, the church itself had a sequestered quality. Palm Sunday was the excuse for the two separate congregations to process from one church to the other, holding little crosses of dried palm leaves which we'd made in Sunday School. My parents grumbled about how 'high' Little St Mary's was, a phrase which didn't make much sense give the diminutive height of the building, but the purple robes of the vicar, the intricate patterns of the traceried windows and above all the perfume of the incense all seemed rather exotic. 'All bells and smells', my father said.

Once when my parents were away and I had been farmed out for the weekend to stay with my train-spotting friend John Sharpe, I was taken to the Round Church, more correctly the Holy Sepulchre. Although this was 'lower', and lacking the incense, it still involved much pageantry and communal chanting of words which everybody except me seemed to know by heart. The building itself was intriguing, especially when told how old it was and the stories of the Knights Templar and their crusades to the Holy Land. It was disappointing years later to find out that the church had been entirely rebuilt in 1841. 'There is not one old stone left' is how Salvin's 'severe restoration' was summarised by Pevsner.

From school we were taken to visit three of Cambridge's oldest ecclesiastic buildings to learn, somewhat succinctly, about architectural history: St Bene't's with its Saxon quoins and arches, Barnwell Priory on Newmarket Road (which indeed seemed very much like a barn) and the tiny redundant St Peter's near the bottom of Castle Hill with its twelfth-century doorway. Not surprisingly in the 1950s and '60s, little attention was given to Victorian architecture. Bodley's masterpiece of All Saints on Jesus Lane, for example, with its rich interior of Kempe, Burne-Jones Ford Madox Brown and William Morris was appreciated by only a few, and known rather irreverently by Jesus College students as 'St Opposites'. It might indeed have been partly demolished in the 1970s save for a vigorous national campaign. Similarly the highly decorated interiors of Jesus and Queens' College Chapels were regarded by my parents as interesting to show to visitors, but essentially gaudy and vulgar.

Other churches and chapels I came to know through concerts rather than through religion. Great St Mary's, the main church of the town, was the venue for a Michaelmas term's worth of organ lesson from Alan Tranah, who was the organist there. Those cold dark Thursday evenings in the organ loft where I would shiver and fumble through an obligatory Bach prelude while my teacher sat smugly in his overcoat and mittens, noisily sucking humbugs, put me off further study of the so-called 'king of instruments' and severely fettered my affection for Great St Mary's, notwithstanding the wonderful views of the city from the top of the tower.

Great St Mary's.

St Andrew's near Petty Cury was used by the Cambridge Tech. orchestra for its concerts, but my favourite place for music became St Edward's, King and Martyr, tucked away between King's Parade and Peas Hill. Hemmed in by narrow alleys and passageways and with steps down into the sunken arcaded nave, St Edward's had an intimacy perfect for chamber music.

King's College Chapel was the unchallenged venue for big concerts, for university, the Cambridge Philharmonic Society, the combined choirs of the local schools, and of course any visiting professional orchestra. It was also the most hallowed and talked-about building in Cambridge. This was perhaps never more so than during the saga of the 'Adoration of the Magi', the uncomfortably large Rubens painting which was donated by Alfred Ernest Allnatt to the college in 1961. Major Allnatt, as he was known professionally, was a property magnate (rather like Colonel Seifert) who spent his spare cash acquiring diamonds and paintings, including the Rubens which he bought in 1959 for £275,000 from the Duke of Westminster, a record price at that time. As many people said then, and will continue to say, if ever there was any building in England not made for it then it was King's College Chapel. For three years it was displayed on an easel in the antechapel, in a corner against the chancel screen. Then, amid great controversy, it was decided that it should form part of the altarpiece at the east end of the choir. Not only did this maximise the clash in style and colours between the baroque oil paints and the magnificent stained-glass windows, but more outrageously, because of the dimensions of the painting the historic fabric was drastically altered including the lowering of the floor and removal of the timber wall panelling. The damage was completed in 1968.

There were not a few who sympathised with the vandals who scratched 'IRA' in 2ft-high letters on the canvas in 1974. I think that even my mother might have, secretly. As recently as 2004 Gavin Stamp described it as, 'One of the greatest aesthetic scandals of the last century.. the cavalier arrogance with which one of the supreme examples of English Perpendicular architecture was treated remains astonishing as well as shocking.'

Wonderful though King's College Chapel is, forgetting the Rubens, it was outshone in my childish eyes by another, Ely Cathedral. For me this mighty galleon sailing proudly in the wide expanse of the Fens was the greatest wonder. Perhaps it was driving north through Cottenham or Waterbeach up onto the Stretham-Wilburton ridge, and seeing the first glimpse through mist of the serrated outline of the west tower and the octagon, or on clear days the distant views from Newmarket Heath when the sun glinted on stone. In Ely itself the cathedral completely dominates the town, from all directions, and with all its monastic relics, the school, the close, the cloisters, the Bishop's Palace, it was like a town in its own right. To me the cathedral seemed both mysterious and miraculous. Why did the west tower, like a magnified version of Great St Mary's, not collapse like the Norman crossing tower had done in 1322? How did Alan of Walsingham manage to raise the eight tall tree trunks to form the lantern as the crown of the massive stone octagon? After smashing up the inside of the Lady Chapel, why did Cromwell's iconoclastic troops not carry on and destroy more?

Unlike the unity of King's College, Ely seemed to have many layers of history and different levels of interest, from the stupendous rhythm of the nave arcades with their varied stone carving to the industrial cylindrical cast-iron heaters. Ely was also luckier with its philanthropists. When a financial crisis in the repair-fund raised the spectre of the cathedral developing the nearby meadows for housing development, John Paul Getty II stepped in and paid the repair bills on the condition that The Paddock should remain undeveloped forever.

They say that Ely Cathedral can be seen from the tower of every parish church in the county, and given the flatness of the landscape I would not doubt it. Some of those parish churches also became familiar landmarks. In a county without the medieval wealth of Suffolk or Norfolk and where low churches with short stumpy towers are the norm, the tall tapering steeples and spires of Willingham, Eltisley, Godmanchester, St Ives, Houghton and Hemingford Abbots stood out as punctuation marks in the countryside. Some were objects of curiosity, such as the bulbous finials on the corners of the battlemented parapets of Cottenham Church or the high pinnacles on the top-heavy tower of Conington near Peterborough, pointed out by my father as a distraction to fractious children in the back seat of the car. So too was the challenge to count as we passed the number of faces of the octagonal and sixteen-sided towers of St Cyriac and St Mary's Churches in Swaffam Priory.

With my young eyes drawn upwards by towers, fan vaulting, octagonal lanterns or sharply pointed steeples, the appreciation of the short and squat or indeed the exquisite gems of Long Stanton, Coton, Boxworth or Hauxton had to wait for a more mature enlightenment.

## SHOPPING

Like most other towns in Britain, shops and shopping in Cambridge have changed more than almost anything else over the last fifty years. Once-familiar Cambridge household names such as Eaden Lilley, Joshua Taylor and Robert Sayle which I regarded when young as institutions which had been and would be there forever, have long gone. In keeping with the rest of the country Cambridge is now awash with the globalised conglomerates who occupy every high street, from Canterbury to Carlisle.

Fifty years ago Cambridge had a compact, well-stocked town centre which served the town and a modest catchment area of surrounding villages. There were also local shopping streets such as Mitcham's Corner and Mill Road, and smaller parades such as the little group halfway along Histon Road, which were our nearest shops.

Shopping, or being dragged around the town centre shops by my mother, was never my favourite activity. At an early age when I was parked in my pram in Sidney Street, I hurled the various items which my mother had just bought in Sainsbury's onto the pavement. This included a tin of Tate and Lyle's Golden Syrup which burst to form a large sticky puddle. Perhaps it gave some meaning to the riddle of the lion and the bees on the tin 'out of the strong came forth sweetness', but it did not amuse my mother who was greatly upset, particularly as food rationing was still in force for such things. Happily, I was later told, an observant and sympathetic shop assistant came out and replaced the tin. Together with Matthews the grocers in Trinity Street, Sainsbury's at that time had old-fashioned service, with two long lines of marble counters down each side of the shop, and you had to queue separately for different items. The whole shop smelled deliciously of smoked bacon and freshly roasted coffee. The ladies behind the counters had their hair tied up under white scarves, and the men wore long brown aprons. The first self-service supermarket was still several years off at that time, yet to arrive from America.

The Eaden Lilley family came to our church. I don't think for a moment that we got any favours from the shop, but my mother liked going there for all sorts of things. The store was big, seemingly occupying much of the frontage on the north side of Market Street, and had grand wide stairs connecting the different departments. My invariable request was to go to the toy department in the basement where there were alluring displays of model railways, including the latest electric oo gauge, Triang and Dinky cars in glass cases, and all sorts of things which we didn't have at home.

Old Mrs Lilley lived in a huge house on the south side of West Road, and the church garden parties were held there. On the expansive lawns we ran egg-and-spoon and three-legged races. To one side there was a pretty coach house where table-tennis or other indoor games could be played if it was wet. In the late 1960s the house and grounds were all subsumed into the university Sidgwick site. The main house survived but the coach house was pulled down for the new Music Faculty and West Road concert hall.

I was too young to remember the celebrations of the 200th anniversary of the founding of Eaden Lilley in the mid-eighteenth century, but it seemed unimaginable that it should ever close. Sadly, of course, it did, in 1999, although the name lives on in Cambridge with the photographic shop in Green Street and the branch stores in Saffron Walden, St Ives and Great Shelford. The old Market Street premises are now WH Smith.

Robert Sayle in St Andrew's Street was considered better for some things, particularly the haberdashery department, with its cotton reels and threads, balls of wool for knitting and endless racks piled with rolls of cloth and material. They did school uniforms for the Perse and the High Schools. There always appeared to be a high degree of bustle and efficiency among the staff. My mother said it was a good place to work because everyone was a 'partner' and shared in the profits. Robert Sayle had indeed been part of the John Lewis Partnership since 1940, having been founded 100 years before that. Now, with the development of the new John Lewis store as part of the huge Grand Arcade development in St Andrew's Street, that old Cambridge name has disappeared, although a section of the façade of the original building has been kept and incorporated.

Most posh, and expensive, was Joshua Taylor's on the corner of Market Street and Sidney Street. Here my father bought his Sunday-best overcoat and Harris Tweed jacket, and fifty years later they still make occasional but respectable outings from my wardrobe. The illuminated row of Christmas trees on the roof of Joshua Taylor's was a familiar December landmark. Its current replacement, Monsoon, is of course typical of the colonisation of England's high street with national multiples.

For hardware, tools, nails and screws, we usually went to Macintosh's ironmongers on Market Hill until they closed in 1962, but for bulkier things for the garden, paint, creosote and brushes we went to Laurie & McConnal's in Fitzroy Street. This had changed little since it opened in 1903. The men who worked there wore long brown coats, exuded a sense of superiority and expected you to know what you wanted. The wooden floorboards were stained and worn, the mahogany counters polished by a thousand leaning elbows. The air was a heady mix of turpentine, paraffin, garden twine, pet food and compost. Laurie's became a victim of the uncertainty over the Kite redevelopment and closed in 1977, but it would never have survived in the modern world of Homebase. Close by in Fitzroy Street was Peake's Furnishers where my parents inspected and bought the utility furniture which stocked our house, simple and 'modern' with no-frills, much more fashionable today than it ever was then. Their proudest acquisition was a blue Parker Knoll arm chair which was considered to be the latest thing in comfort and back support. Climbing or jumping onto it was strictly forbidden. Peake's, together with lots of other local shops in Burleigh Street and Fitzroy Street, disappeared under the new shopping 'experience' of the Grafton Centre, which thirty years on now too seems dated and tired. Laurie's building did survive, with its curious 'bandstand' cupola on the roof, and was decently refurbished by Habitat.

For everyday clothes, my mother rarely deviated from Marks & Spencer's in Sidney Street. Their shop had a shining chrome front, with large plate glass windows and easy swing doors which let in lots of light and fresh air. I wondered whether their 'St Michael' name tag gave their merchandise some divine advantage over their rivals. My mother disapproved strongly when they started selling food, thinking that it would never mix with clothes.

Cambridge, like Oxford, traditionally had an abundance of small and rather expensive menswear shops, feeding the university's appetite for college scarves and ties, blazers, boaters, gowns and dinner jackets. A few have gone, such as Buttress & Co. in St John Street, Bodgers in

Sidney Street and Roper & Sons in Trinity Street, but many more survive. Hardy & Amies in King's Parade, James Neal on the corner of Silver Street and Trumpington Street (now renamed Ede & Ravenscroft), A.E Clothier, Giles and Arthur Shepherd all seem to exist exclusively on this trade. Town folk like us never visited them. Probably tourists as much as students keep them going today.

Sometimes, in search of a bargain, we called in at Mitcham's department store at the junction of Chesterton Road and Victoria Avenue. Although there were other local shops along Chesterton Road, this was an odd place for a big shop and it never looked very busy compared to the main town centre shops. When my parents first arrived in Cambridge, Mitcham's is where they bought their first pram. My mother probably retained a sentimental attachment.

The corner building was single storey, and rather shack-like, with a roof-top sign on the bend saying 'Mitcham's Corner'. Inside there were cheap clothes, nylon shirts, string vests and imported shoes, and acres of net curtains. The most exciting event was in 1960 when an articulated lorry crashed into the front of the shop. Perhaps it was that which helped to promote the traffic scheme which in 1967 resulted in a new one-way gyratory which marooned several properties in the central island. It didn't do much to help Mitcham's which closed in 1977, a bad year for Edwardian shops in Cambridge. It is now a sports shop.

We got our meat from a butcher in Milton Road, and occasionally from another in Victoria Road. In the 1950s and '60s there were small independent butchers everywhere, although chains such as Dewhurst & Matthews began to take over in the city centre. Big sides of beef and pork hanging from hooks, piles of red mince in open trays, dishes filled with ox tongues, lambs' kidneys and chicken livers, and sawdust on the floors were then the norm. It was no surprise when we had to dissect a cow's eye as part of our biology O-Level exam at school that they should be brought in a big bucket by one of the class, Rob Badcock, whose father worked in Gilbert's butchers in Botolph Lane.

Cambridge market was a very ordinary and quite small affair, and was used much of the time as a car park with stalls only around the outside. Most of these sold fruit and veg and were run by local market gardeners. My mother would use them to augment whatever Mr Wiseman didn't have. Only towards the end of the 1960s did greater diversity arrive, such as Andy's Records, a book stall selling cheap Penguin paperbacks, and traders selling cheese-cloth shirts, denim jeans, hippy flares and cotton loons. The present-day mix of organic olives, 'world' cheeses, hand made bread, ethnic fast-food, craft knick-knacks and bric-a-brac were inconceivable then.

The town centre also had its specialist traders, many very long established. W. Heffer & Sons Ltd., the bookseller, was in Petty Cury and next to the original Sainsbury on Sidney Street before it moved to much larger and smarter premises in Trinity Street in 1970. On the corner of Trinity Street and Market Street was Bowes & Bowes bookshop, today just another branch of Heffer's, which in turn was taken over by Blackwell's of Oxford. With some sensitivity to Cambridge pride they at least kept the Heffer's name. Amazingly Galloway & Porter has survived as a family-run student bookshop in Sidney Street, resisting all take-over attempts.

Jarrolds, the stationers, was next to Joshua Taylor on Market Street, and was where we bought Quink ink for our pens, envelopes and writing paper. In those days Boots on the corner of Sidney Street and Petty Cury was a chemist and nothing much more. Our bank was the Midland, now HSBC, which occupied the ground floor of the new King's College student hostel in Peas Hill. This had replaced the old Central Temperance Hotel, which had been demolished with some protests in 1959.

My father bought his beloved Ilford camera and Agfa film from Campkins who still have shops in Rose Crescent, Market Street and King's Parade. Hobbs sports shop was in Trinity Street, now relocated to Sidney Street. Today they sell a very wide range of sporting equipment

Fitzbillies in Trumpington Street.

and clothing, but in the 1950s there was an exclusive emphasis on university games, such as squash rackets, hockey sticks and cricket bats. My father sometimes took me inside to look at the latest Gray-Nicholls models, fresh from their factory in Benson Street just off the top of Huntingdon Road near Murkett's garage. Hayward's on Trumpinton Street sold and mended bikes, as they still do, and for other bits and pieces there was Halford's on the corner of Bridge Street and Jesus Lane, still there today. King & Harpers' car showroom was also in Bridge Street (as well as their main workshop at Hills Road) and further down Jesus Lane was Marshall's car repair premises where my father took the car for servicing.

A little old man with a leather apron and bottle-thick glasses mended and re-soled our shoes from a tiny shop in Victoria Road. Even smaller was the watch-mender's garret behind Corn Exchange Street. His historic hovel in St Tibb's Row, together with the Bun Shop pub and many other ancient buildings, were swept away for the ghastly Lion Yard shops and car park in the early 1970s.

Millers, who claimed to be the second oldest music shop in the country, were in Sidney Street, and rather snootily had a monopoly on pianos and piano tuners. They were unchallenged until old Mr Woolfenden, father of the illustrious Guy, opened the Cambridge Music Shop in All Saints Passage in the 1960s, and Ken Stevens opened their music instrument shop in Hobson Street. For all Mr Woolfenden's grumpiness, his shop had an arty and free-spirited quality. It was sad when he died and the shop closed, to be replaced by a restaurant. Now Millers and Ken Stevens too are merged, and trading in Sussex Street. The Garon book and record shop in King Street, where students spent happy hours rummaging for bargains, is another loss.

For a treat on a Saturday, after an organ recital at King's, my father might have deviated via Fitzbillies in Trumpington Street to buy Chelsea buns, dripping with sugary syrup. Thankfully at least that survives, rebuilt after the fire in 1998. So does the small chemist further along past Pembroke College, now Lloyds but still with its distinctive Peck's sign on the corner. They were one of the town's chemists who took it in turns to open on Sundays.

Our nearest shopping parade, halfway along Histon Road, provided an unremarkable range – Vernon Allen the chemist, Clarke's tobacconist and newsagent, Underwoods ironmonger, Gary's electrical, Achille Serre dry cleaners, Taverners greengrocer and Windsor shoe repairs – typical of any post-war suburban shopping street. We called the chemist 'Mr Thank-you-very-much' because he said it so often. In the late 1950s Adkins grocers was replaced by a new International Stores, which my mother liked as a convenient alternative to Sainsbury's in the town, and with shorter queues. That closed in 1969 and was replaced by a Co-op. The greengrocer was replaced by Peatling & Cauldron wine merchants. Exton's fish and chip shop at No.113 Histon Road which we patronised every Friday evening survived longer than most. For a while it was renamed the Frying Pan, and it's still there, even with some of the original tiles on the shop front, but now it's called KFS and has been gutted and re-ordered inside. None of the takeaways now, of course, are allowed to be wrapped in newspaper; instead we have to put up with bulky plastic and polystyrene containers.

# FENLAND

The Fens are an acquired taste, probably best infused as a child when adulation or criticism of landscape is low on the agenda. With repeated exposure to their endless low horizons and vast skies the Fens do, eventually, take on a stark beauty of their own.

My father's job with the Great Ouse River Board, which eventually became part of Anglian Water, involved ensuring the successful drainage of the low-lying land which we call the Fens. Following the catastrophic floods of 1947 when hundreds of people perished, and again in 1953, sizeable government funds were allocated to flood protection to prevent a repeat of such calamities. GORB's headquarters were in a large detached Victorian house called Elmhurst on Brooklands Avenue but from 1965 they relocated in an impressive new office block, now known as Lockton House, in Clarendon Road just off the Hills Road end of Brooklands Avenue behind what then were the warehouse premises of Pordages fruit and vegetables merchants.

My father inspecting drainage work at Stretham catchwater, September 1964. (Author's Collection)

At least one day a week my father would have to go out to see or supervise works which were being carried out, and in the school holidays there was always the possibility of going too, armed with a packed lunch.

For me every trip was an adventure, an opportunity to escape the immediate confines of our house and garden, and the chance to sit in the front passenger seat of the car.

The catchment area of the Great Ouse River and its tributaries is huge, not only the vast flat fens between Cambridge and the Wash, but large tracts of Norfolk, Suffolk, Bedfordshire and Buckinghamshire and parts of Northamptonshire, Lincolnshire, Hertfordshire and even into Oxfordshire. While the big engineering projects were major schemes such as installing new main gates and lifting gear to Denver Sluice or new electric pumping stations to replace steam or diesel, we would sometimes go to the upper reaches where blocked streams or malfunctioning weirs were causing local problems with farmers or land owners. Usually my father would have arranged to see someone from the contractors or a representative of the local drainage board. Everyone was referred to solely by their surname, not even Mr so-and-so. My father always introduced himself simply as 'Forshaw', and his colleagues in the River Board were 'Chalcraft', 'Scudamore' or 'Doran' (his boss). I of course had no part in these meetings and might stay in the car or walk along a river bank or the edge of a drainage dyke. Sometimes there would be huge draglines on caterpillar tracks scooping mud and silt in big metal buckets from the water and forming raw angled sides to the channel. The smell of fresh earth piled high and the ooze from the river beds would mix with the fumes from the engine exhausts. Sometimes on the freshly ploughed fields there would be flocks of lapwings and godwits, or on the flooded marshes heron, grebe, snipe or bittern. Skeins of Whooper or Bewick swans formed irregular 'V' formations in the sky.

Naturally I was frequently indoctrinated about the exploits of Vermuyden and the Duke of Bedford who had devised and carried out the extraordinary endeavours of New and Old Bedford rivers, the so-called 'hundred foot drain'. There was also the great conundrum that, as the Fens were successfully drained, so the fertile peat soil for which the farmers craved dried out and shrank, which lowered the land still further below sea level. This required more pumping of water from the fields up into the dykes and rivers which needed higher and higher banks, and brought greater risk of flooding. How might it all end, I sometimes wondered. One day the peat will run out, my father would say, and then the lucrative carrot and pea crops would be gone too.

Nowhere did this seem to be more alarmingly illustrated than at the Holme post near Peterborough. Here in 1852 when the ancient Whittlesey Mere was drained, a long iron post was sunk deep into the ground right through the peat, with its base embedded into the clay below and with its top left level with the surface. As the peat oxidised and was blown away so more and more of the post was revealed; it and its adjacent 1950s replica now stand about 15ft above the ground.

Holme Fen with it silver birch woods and narrow lanes was one of my favourite trips, not least because it was bisected by the main railway line to the north. I was perfectly happy to be left for an hour or two while my father went off to inspect a pumping station or drainage ditch. It was a thrill to watch the express trains with their liveried Pullman coaches and romantic names tearing past, *The West Riding*, *The White Rose*, *The Master Cutler*, *The Queen of Scots*. They were pulled then still by the great and famous steam engines, like 'Mallard', 'Sir Nigel Gresley', 'The Dominion of New Zealand' and 'The Flying Scotsman', and also by the new diesel-electric 'Deltics' which were named after regiments and racehorses.

On one occasion at the tiny level crossing just north of Holme, my father and his fellow engineer Chalcraft placed a new penny on the line and we watched in amazement as the passing carriages flatted the coin into a thin disc five times as big. Near Conington a single-track road ran

Reach Lode, as normal. (Author's Collection)

for a mile directly alongside the railway, and it was a good place in wet weather to sit in the car, eat our sandwiches and watch the trains thunder by. There was also a signal box where you could see the man pulling the huge levers before and after each and every train went by.

It was a surprise when late one autumn evening in 1963 there was knock on our back door at home and two policemen came in to question my father. Our car had been spotted and the registration noted at Conington a few days earlier in the autumn half-term holiday by the signalman, who had observed my father and I as we watched and took down the numbers of trains. Such as isolated spot might indeed have been a good place for a second Great Train Robbery. Fortunately we had a good alibi for 8 August when the actual heist happened as we were in Wales on holiday.

Part of the atmosphere of the Fens comes not only from its man made unnaturalness, with its dead-straight roads, rivers and dykes, the huge black fields and a horizontal horizon, broken only by power pylons or Ely Cathedral, but from the weird and wonderful names. Where else in England do you find such strange places as Mepal and Manea, Upwell and Outwell, Southery and Oxlode, Botany Bay and Delph Bridge, Sawtry and Warboys? Even the towns have odd names such as Chatteris, Wisbech and March. At Prickwillow I was once told, probably apocryphally, that half the inhabitants had the surname Gotobed. It was certainly a Fenland name, and used by Dorothy L. Sayers in *The Nine Tailors*.

Often the villages straggle along the higher ground of the drainage banks, safer no doubt except for dangers of subsidence. Below the dykes were the low flat expanses of farmland – Decoy Fen, Black Fen, Burnt Fen, Grime Fen and Adventurers Fen – names which recalled the old Fenland practices of fishing and hunting wildfowl from before Vermuyden's reclamation, when in warm wet weather some areas were malaria-infested swamps. The drains and rivers had a curious mixture of prosaic names, such as the Twenty Foot River, Middle Level Main Drain, or Sixteen Foot Drain, and the more evocative, such as the Old West River, Grunty Fen Drain, Welches Dam, Reach Lode or Hermitage Lock. Even the names of some of the long straight roads had stories to tell, such as Parsons Drove and the Twenty Pence Road.

Occasionally I met some of the gnarled old men and women who looked after the locks, weirs and pumps. They were a rum and weather-beaten lot, hardly surprising considering their lonely existence and the windy damp rheumatic conditions which they had to endure. It never appealed as a future career opportunity.

We did sometimes go on family trips to the fens, when my father would take some pride in showing us some new pumping station which he had been working on. At Houghton we would walk across the water meadows from Hemingford Abbots to see the new weir, and the great wooden water wheel at the side of the old black timber mill. At Ely we would walk along the towpath beside the river and look at all the new lock gates and house boats. At Earith we sometimes had to drive through shallow floodwater which had encroached across the road, and sometimes turn back if the water looked too deep. Whenever we went through St Ives we were regaled with the riddle, 'As I was going to St Ives I met a man with seven wives; each wife had seven sacks, each sack had seven cats, each cat had seven kits; how many were going to St Ives?' The answer, of course, was one, because the others were all leaving St Ives.

My father became involved with the preservation of the Stretham Old Engine which was a steam-powered beam engine dating from 1831 which stood beside the Great Ouse near Ely. With its tall chimney and industrial brick engine shed this was a frequent family excursion, and a real thrill if it was working. Inside the engine house we would stand deafened as the huge beam was hurled back and forth and the giant flywheel was spun round at a frightening speed by it strong wide belts. I was always worried that such immense power might get out of control and cause the whole mechanism to break loose. It seemed amazing that this mighty leviathan, which had replaced the work of four windmills should itself have been superseded by a modest electric pump in a building only a tenth of its size.

Sometimes we went on to nearby Wicken Fen where there were historic windmills and lots of reed beds and marshes which, we were told, was what the Fens used to be like everywhere before Vermuyden. Maybe they will again, if the long-term plans of the National Trust to expand Wicken Fen come to fruition and if elsewhere it is decided to relax the flood defences and allow the rising sea to inundate the lowest-lying land. There are plans between Huntingdon and Peterborough to link the two existing nature reserves at Holme Fen and Woodwalton to create what would be known as the Great Fen. At 3,700 hectares this would be the largest wetland habitat in Britain. Perhaps then at last the marsh harriers, so rare for much of the twentieth century, will rule the skies again over Cambridgeshire.

Wicken Lode,
29 December 1962.
(Author's Collection)

# BEDFORD

Bedford was an hour away by car, and because of my grandmother was almost a second home. The journey was familiar and routine – out along the Madingley Road, up the hill past the American Cemetery, crossing Ermine Street or the A14 at Caxton Gibbet, winding through Eltisley, sometimes with cricket on the village green, crawling through St Neots, joining the Great North Road for a few miles at Eaton Socon, and then the last leg through Roxton and Great Barford to the outskirts of Bedford. The billowing steam from the multiple cooling towers of the power station at Little Barford, the regular gypsy encampment on the roadside verge at Croxton and the neatly grazed straight undersides to the trees in Croxton Hall park were landmarks and talking points.

My grandmother was known to nearly everyone as 'Ga'. This apparently was the nearest that my brother Roger could get as an infant to pronouncing 'grandma', and being the first grandchild this simplification had a universal appeal. She lived in Newnham Avenue which was an extension of the Embankment leading up to the Goldington Road. The Embankment was, and still is, one of Bedford's more desirable spots, running alongside the River Ouse. No. 10 where she lived was a large semi-detached house, very near the river, but well set back from the road, and with allotment gardens opposite.

The Embankment with its ornamental gardens and weeping willows, its elegant curved pedestrian suspension bridge and the boating lakes and recreation grounds beyond, was a stone's throw from the house. From the earliest trips in a pram to feed the ducks and swans to teenage outings in canoes and rowing boats, this was an obvious and frequent playground.

Compared to Cambridge the town centre of Bedford in the 1950s had a very compact and rather commercial quality, and lots of through traffic. Until the M1 was opened many lorries still used the old A6, straight through the middle of Bedford over the old bridge and up the High Street. Most of the buildings were grimy red brick, very different to the pale Burwell brick of Cambridge, and the posh imported stones for the university colleges. Few of the buildings in

The suspension bridge and Embankment, Bedford 1962. (Author's Collection)

the centre were imposing, certainly nothing on the scale of Cambridge's University Library or King's Chapel. Even the parish church of St Peter's seemed to have an almost rural quality, set back off a little green behind the statue of John Bunyan. Bedford however did have a gaol with high brick walls and on the outskirts big factories, such as Vauxhall's car works, and most noticeably, at least in one's nostrils, the brick works. Whenever the wind was from the south-west then the sulphurous smoke from the dozens of chimneys in the brick fields at Stewartby would waft across Bedford.

Before the war 'Ga' had lived in Pemberley Avenue in an even grander house near the town park. The subsequent conversion of this house, and most of the others in the street into flats, and their occupation by Italians and Indians, who had come to work in the brick furnaces, was a regular subject of complaint. Rose-tinted spectacles were readily available even then.

The house in Newnham Avenue had plenty of bedrooms, enough for us all to stay, every room furnished with ornate and musty Victorian furniture and heavy drape curtains. As well as the large sitting room and dining room there was a parlour off the kitchen with large clock which ticked with a resonant clonk. On the top attic floor lived the lodger, Barbara Wagg, who was a stout and cheerful single lady and who was a good companion for my grandmother to have around.

If we were there on a Sunday we would go to Bunyan Meeting in Mill Street for the morning service. My parents had a sentimental affection for the place, having been married there, but I found it cold and forbidding. The box pews with their gates felt like a prison and sitting as we did on one side, the galleries above us on their cast-iron columns seemed uncomfortably low. I liked the tune of Bunyan's hymn, 'He who would valiant be', but otherwise the place conjured up the Slough of Despond rather than the Delectable Mountains or the Celestial City.

Bedford was famous for its schools, not just the fee-paying Bedford School, but also the Bedford Modern and the High Schools, where my mother and her sister had gone. Sport was a major part of the curriculum and my grandmother loved to watch the rowing eights practising on the river and we would often walk across to the boathouses to watch them disembarking. The Bedford regatta was her highlight of the year.

In the 1950s and '60s Bedford had a good rugby club and it played and did well against other top English teams. My father had even played for them when he was an apprentice in Bedford, and keenly followed their results. Several times we went to watch them at their ground in Goldington Road. Many of our visits to Bedford also involved a trip to see my aunt Barbara, uncle Sidney and cousins David and Angela out in Oakley, a village about four miles north along the A6. They lived in a small nineteenth-century stone cottage, at the end of a terrace in Station Road, and they backed onto the main railway line which was in a deep cutting. Rather like the Railway Children we would stand on the timber post-and-rail fence and wave at the trains as they passed. When I was in my trainspotting phase it was an exciting opportunity to see the different engines of the London Midland Scottish line, and the express trains from St Pancras in their maroon livery.

The cottage itself was small and pokey, full of cigarette smoke and the smell of their Scotty dog, Sooty. Downstairs there were just two rooms, a kitchen and parlour, with the stairs running straight up from behind a simple plank door. Originally the outside lavatory was the other side of the clinker track which ran along the length of the terrace at the back. Sometime in the 1960s, little brick ground floor bathroom extensions were built, probably by the Council who had taken over as freeholders from the Duke of Bedford's estate, Much later, when my grandmother was in her nineties, still driving, but showing some signs of ageing, the cottage immediately next door came up for sale, and rather regrettably it was decided that she should move in.

It was a mistake. Ga hated it there and sorely missed her old house in Newnham Avenue and her Bedford friends. In Oakley she felt cut off, and was constantly nagged and irritated by the proximity of her daughter and son-in-law, without any of the benefit of seeing more of her grandchildren who had by then long left home, in rather bad odour.

Most of my strongest impressions of Bedford came from the stories and reminiscences of my grandmother. She came from a well-to-do family of Bedford shopkeepers, the Covingtons, and despite her grumbles she had a fierce pride in Bedford. She would recall fondly how in 1941 the BBC Symphony Orchestra were evacuated to Bedford and broadcast their concerts from Bedford School and the Corn Exchange. The players were billeted with local families, including a few in her house.

Her own grandmother, who my mother referred to as 'Granny Covington', had been one of the grand old ladies of Bedford. In her old age she had ridden a tricycle and used to leave it in the middle of the road if she wanted to go into a shop. She was riding this very machine when aged 102 she had a 'seizure' and died.

The main bone of resentment with my grandmother was that when her father died, the family fortune had been left entirely to her solitary brother, Wallace, who had eventually left Bedford and went to live on the Sussex coast. They were not on the best terms. The mystery of her own husband's fate was never mentioned, let alone explained.

Because of her age, her colourful character and her unusual career on the buses and running a driving school, she knew a huge number of people in the town. When she was in her eighties she was shown a photograph taken in 1915 of seventy-four recruits for the Bedfordshire Regiment; she could name over sixty of the men, and say a lot more besides about many of them and their families. Most of these young lads never returned from France or Gallipoli. That and the fact that she outlived so many of her other contemporaries was an unhappiness to her.

There was, however, a far greater sadness, carefully controlled and coped with as only the British can. In the hall, on the mantelpiece in the lounge and on the sideboard in the dining room of my grandmother's house were photographs of a fresh faced young man, resplendent in his RAF uniform, displaying his 'wings'. Michael, her only son and my mother's brother, had been killed in Germany at the end of the war on his twenty-fourth birthday. Nobody ever said much to me as a child about it, even when I asked, but his death cast a shadow over everything.

Sometimes we would drive home to Cambridge by a different route, through Sandy and Poton. This took us past the massive twin hangers at Cardington, built to take the vast cigar shapes of the R100 and R101. Having seen pictures in a *Boys' Own* annual of the Hindenburg disaster and been told about the doomed first flight of the R101, Cardington had a rather menacing quality and I found the whole idea of airships terrifying. It was always something of a relief to see the comforting names of Wreslingworth and Gamlingay and to pass the great double avenue of elms and oaks at Wimpole as we came back into Cambridge along the Barton Road.

## ALL THOSE OTHER AUNTS AND UNCLES

A curious part of my early childhood was the realisation that many of the adults who were known to me as 'aunts' or 'uncles' were in fact no such thing, and were simply friends of my parents. There was of course nothing particularly unusual about this. In the 1950s it might have been considered disrespectful for a child to call an adult simply by their Christian name. The prefix of 'uncle' or 'aunt' made it acceptable. The alternative was to call them Mr or Mrs, which seemed somewhat Victorian. It was unthinkable to call one's own parents by their Christian names, and I remember being quite shocked when told at school that some families did this, rather than calling them 'mum' and 'dad'.

Our amiable neighbours on the other side of the Histon Road, the Maskells, were 'Uncle Claud' and 'Uncle Cyril' to me. In Bedford the two elderly ladies who lived in a grand but fusty detached house in Kimbolton Road, and who were good friends of my grandmother, were 'Auntie Dorie' and 'Auntie May'. These well-heeled but starchy sisters were particularly doting on my brother who had had the dubious fortune or misfortune of being taken with them and my grandmother for Easter holidays at Clacton. Dorothy and Mabel, to use their proper names, were spinsters and no doubt regarded poor Roger as a surrogate nephew or great-nephew.

Auntie Pip and Uncle Buster were friends of my parents and altogether more fun and glamorous. Pip had been a bosom pal of my mother when they were both young and single and sharing a flat in London before the war. Her real name was Mary, but Pip was a playground nickname which had stuck for good. I never knew what Buster's real Christian was, but his surname was Humm, and the combination of Buster Humm had a convincing and reassuring ring to it.

They were both short, neither of them much above 5ft tall, but nonetheless they were very elegant, Pip as petite as a doll, and Buster always dapper and nattily dressed, with his hair slicked back with Brylcreme and a parting as straight as a ruler. They didn't have children and seemed to have led an exotic and almost nomadic life. For several years they had lived in Africa in Tanganyika and Kenya, where Buster had been involved in designing and constructing schools and prisons. When they returned they had tried several ventures, including running a local shop and post office in a small village on the Somerset Levels. When they retired they moved to Donyatt just outside Chard, and I spent a few days with them when revising for my O-Levels. They visited us quite frequently, usually in the summer, and Buster was always keen to watch some cricket at Fenner's. Because our house didn't have a spare bedroom they would usually have to stay in a bed and breakfast somewhere in town.

Auntie Janet, or Janet Stirling, was the widow of a colleague of my father's in India, and she lived in Craigendoran, west of Glasgow on the north bank of the River Clyde close to Helensburgh. Living in a spacious three-storey house on her own she had plenty of room for guests and we always stayed with her when we went to Scotland. She spoke with a soft lilting Scottish accent and had the most kindly manner, her grey hair neatly tied in a bun, and her woollen cardigan or tartan shawl on chilly evenings always fastened with the same large silver thistle broach.

Auntie Lorna and Uncle Tom were my favourites. Tom was the brother of Sidney, who was the husband of my mother's sister Barbara. They too had no children and shared a small terraced house with Lorna's brother, Jack, just a few streets away from my grandmother in Bedford. Lorna and Tom had an unquenchable enthusiasm for life, and both had infectious laughs, Tom's a high-pitched chortle and Lorna's a throaty cackle. Tom kept bees, and in order to be able to have more hives they moved out to the delightful village of Harrold, about ten miles north of Bedford to a house with a big back garden which looked onto fields. Tom was also mad about cricket and they would come over to Fenner's, usually to watch a touring team play the university. Tom also shared my father's enthusiasm for tape recorders and cameras, and classical music.

As well as his elder brother John, my father had a younger brother George. Uncle George and Auntie Gladys lived with their four children on the outskirts of York in an ordinary 1930s semi from which George ran his own wholesale business selling what my mother described as 'fancy goods'. These seemed to comprise an odd mix of toiletries, cosmetics and trinkets, and George spent most of his time driving around Yorkshire selling the stuff from the back of his car. Gladys and daughter Ann did the books from their home. Every Christmas we would receive a hurriedly packed parcel containing a selection of these knick-knacks, invariably in gaudy plastic. The three other cousins were boys, and all spoke with a strong Yorkshire dialect which I found hard to understand. I can't remember them all visiting us in Cambridge, probably because George never stopped working (except for a one week holiday every August when they went to Scarborough) and because it would have been a squash to get the whole family into the car. So we occasionally visited them instead, usually calling in to their cramped and untidy house if we were on our way to Scotland. Both George and Gladys smoked like chimneys, and the house reeked of stale cigarettes. It did for them both when they reached their sixties.

My mother kept in close contact with her own cousins, despite the rifts between the older generation of the family, and this thus provided another tier of 'aunts' and 'uncles'. From her father's brother's side there was Auntie Margaret, a prim spinster nurse who lived in Spalding (the ancestral home of the Gooches), and Auntie Mary who was married to Paul, a Wisbech doctor. Auntie Margaret was sternly alert, fastidious and incredibly organised, whereas her sister Mary was giggly, light-headed and disorganised. I don't believe I ever saw the two of them together.

My grandmother's brother Wallace had three children, all educated and elocuted at English boarding schools in the 1930s. Sheila and Stuart emigrated to Canada, married, had families, and lived in considerable style and comfort. Sheila and her amiable husband Bob (a pioneer in nickel mining) usually took in Cambridge on their frequent European tours. They would stay at the University Arms or the Garden House Hotel and pay us a visit for tea. This would involve getting out the best china and silver teaspoons from the bottom of the sideboard, doilies for the cake stand and a silver bowl of sugar lumps with tweezers instead of the usual loose sugar. My mother was keen to put on the best possible display, perhaps to show that despite everything we in England hadn't done too badly after all.

The third, Uncle Ian Covington, was an airline pilot, and although he lived in Weybridge Surrey, we saw very little of him. This was a shame because he had the most alluring *Boys' Own* story, having been a bomber pilot in the war. He had been shot down over France, eluded the Germans by hiding in pigsties and haystacks and, with the help of the French Resistance, escaped over the Pyrenees to Spain where a British submarine brought him home. This was jaw-dropping stuff for any impressionable child, particularly in a family where wartime memories were strongly repressed.

All things considered these aunts and uncles, real or not, were a motley collection, and I should be thankful to my parents for having such a variety of friends and relatives. They opened up a wider vision of a world outside Cambridge than I probably appreciated at the time.

Picnic at Brown's Woods on my grandmother's seventy-fifth birthday, May 1963. (Author's Collection)

# SCHOOL PART I

When I was five I started at my first school, Milton Road Infant/Junior, which was on the corner of Milton Road and Gilbert Road. The infants, taking children up to the age of seven, occupied the block facing Gilbert Road and had exclusive use of the grassy play area between the school buildings and the first house in Gilbert Road, which was set back behind a very deep front garden. The play space had a small sandpit on a worn bit of grass and a little copse of shrubs and young silver birch trees. The older children, the 'juniors', had the larger tarmac playground facing Milton Road. Behind the school were the stands and floodlights of the Cambridge City football ground.

The school buildings were pretty, Edwardian red-brick with clay tile roofs, and big multi-paned timber windows which let in plenty of light. Nearly everything was done in the main hall: assembly, lessons, lunch and games if it was too wet to play outside. The whole school smelt of an unpleasant mixture of floor polish and boiled cabbage. This intensified when the noisy roller shutter was cranked up at dinner time to reveal the fetid kitchen where the cabbage was being boiled to death. It is perhaps not surprising that my memories of my two years at Milton Road are not of the lessons but the horrors and anxieties of school dinners. On one occasion with my cheeks stuffed with inedible meat, my request to go to the lavatory meant that I was accompanied by a teacher who made sure that I didn't spit out the unchewable gristle. It was only later that I managed to slip the offending lumps into the pocket of my trousers. Such experiences can be deeply harrowing, and the fear of being served tough meat remains.

My mother took and fetched me on her bicycle, which was a journey I always enjoyed, perched on my seat at the front. One afternoon at half past three, a girl in my class called Sandra was hit by a lorry as she ran across Gilbert Road immediately outside the school. I remember her lying there quite still, wearing her red cardigan, and then a crowd of people and an ambulance. My mother said that she had banged her head, but I never saw her again.

The school and its environs have changed greatly since then. Next to the Cambridge City football ground, an architecturally undistinguished business park, the Westbrook Centre, was developed in the 1990s. The City Ground itself is now under threat. More sadly, in 2007 the old school was demolished despite local protestations about its architectural merit and suitability for retention and conversion to another use. A new larger school with spacious playing fields has now been built on the Ascham Road sports ground. The flattened old site is now being redeveloped; only the fading green railings remain in front of the hoardings and a fragment of the little spinney of now mature silver birches, where over the decades thousands children must have played.

Aged seven it was decided, as with my brother before me, that rather than continuing into the Milton Road Junior School, which had a dubious reputation, I should go to the Perse Preparatory School, three miles away in Trumpington Road. This was a fee-paying day school which took boys from seven to eleven. There were no boarders, unlike the nearby St Faith's which was the prep school for the Leys School and took boys up to the age of thirteen, but it did include lessons on Saturday mornings. It was too far for my mother to take me and I was not old enough to cycle on my own. However it wasn't a big detour for my father, working in Brooklands Avenue, to drop me at the Porson Road entrance in the morning, although I had to take the bus home.

When I started in September 1958 the annual fee was £72, with school dinner 1s 9d. By the following year this had gone up to £102 per annum, and by September 1961 to £114. Even though this was about 10 per cent of my father's income my parents clearly thought it was worth it, and that this was the best time to inject some of their precious money into their offspring's education.

Compared to Milton Road Infants, the Perse Prep was spacious, and blessed with wonderful grounds. The school itself occupied a large red-brick mansion, a rather imposing building with

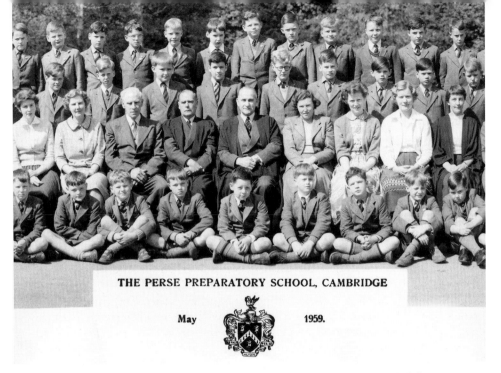

**THE PERSE PREPARATORY SCHOOL, CAMBRIDGE**

May 1959.

Perse Preparatory School, 1959. Mr Stubbs is in the centre, Mr Lindeman immediately left, Miss Carmichael is second from the far left. (Panora Films)

prominent bays and gables and stone dressing to the windows. Originally called Leighton House, it was built in 1865 for Robert Sayle, who had previously been living over his shop in the town centre. He had done so well in his business that he could now afford a fine new detached villa in the fields between the town and Trumpington village. He and his large family and servants lived there for twenty-five years but it was then bought by the Perse as a house for senior school boarders. The Prep had been founded in 1910 and occupied premises in Bateman Street until 1950 when they moved into Leighton House, and the boarders moved to Glebe Road, off Hills Road.

Robert Sayle was clearly keen on trees and planted native and exotic specimens with great foresight. The mature sequoias, or Wellingtonias as we called them, copper beech and horse chestnuts stand to this day like giants on the generous expanse of grass. These were superb grounds for sport and play, formal and informal, and everyone looked forward to break-time.

The master-in-charge, for that was his title, was Mr Hugh Lindeman, a rather fierce man of whom I and most of my fellow pupils (and probably some of the teachers too) were petrified. He smoked a pipe, had lots of nasal hair and in his black gown and mortar board taught us Maths and Latin, although I found the latter a very bewildering experience. Starting languages early is a good idea in principle, and I enjoyed my first assays at French, but Latin is a bit tough.

I found the lady teachers far more sympathetic. Everybody's favourite was Miss Carmichael who taught English and Art for thirty years from 1945 to 1975, and inspired thousands of eager young minds and imaginations. Miss Taylor and Miss Bedford were lovely too, and nature study was a highlight, collecting and pressing leaves, conkers and beech nuts, and keeping stick insects in glass jars. Even the stricter Mrs Spence, who organised the clubs and sports, had her softer side. With her shrill whistle, hung on a ribbon round her neck, I learnt first-aid, semaphore, navigation, cycle proficiency, and all the other badge-collecting activities which culminated in becoming a 'sixer'. Despite all that, I never did understand the 'dyb-dyb-dyb, dob-dob-dob' mantra, although I found out that it was an acronym for 'Do Your Best, Do Our Best'. The woggles, scarves, garters and caps were all rather strange too. I am quite glad that I never went on to become a scout.

For sport we were divided into three 'houses', Barbarians (red), Foresters (green) and Corinthians (blue), and competitive athletics, football and cricket were greatly encouraged. The school certainly took itself seriously. The uniform of vertical purple, black and white stripes for the blazers and caps was smart and eye-catching (and expensive). Speech Day and Sports Day were big occasions attended by most parents. On those red-letter days we would go to the senior school in Hills Road, an opportunity to glimpse their even more formidable headmaster, Mr Stanley Stubbs.

More important than these new rituals were the friends I made, for the first time boys of my own age and who weren't near neighbours. My closest new buddies were Charles Wellington, who lived in Teversham and whose father was head of the National Institute of Agriculture and Botany (NIAB) in Huntingdon Road, and John Tebbit, whose family were farmers in Toft, and together we formed a 'gang of three'. Often we visited each other's houses, and the fields, woods and farm tracks of Toft and Teversham became new adventure playgrounds. For many years John came on holiday with us, because his parents were busy on the farm during the August harvest. With Charles and his family I went to Cornwall for the first time to stay with his great-uncle in Gorran Haven. I don't know why the three of us got on so well. Perhaps it was because in our own families we experienced a similar place in the pecking order, each with one sibling several years older than us, which gave us a shared outlook on life and a natural bond.

Apart from my illness, when I missed seventy days of school in the spring of 1960, these were happy times, truly carefree. I vaguely remember an exam in the last year which my parents said was called the eleven-plus, and was probably combined with an entrance test for the upper Perse school. I don't recall any revision or sense of pressure or stress. In all likelihood not much has changed at the Perse Prep in that respect. There have been new buildings, and in 2008 a sleek black and white glass box has been completed (by Sheppard Robson architects) on the little grass knoll at the south end, housing a new hall, music and sports facilities. Since September 2007 the school has taken girls, and undoubtedly there is now a greater ethnic diversity than was the case fifty years ago; but little boys wearing purple and black striped blazers and carrying leather satchels still arrive at 9.00 a.m and leave at 3.30 p.m with all the enthusiasm of old, and the mighty trees still guard the green sward.

# HEALTH

I was, unfortunately, a rather sickly child, and thus had more contact with doctors and hospital than might be considered desirable. I was delivered as a baby in the Mill Road Maternity Hospital, which I discovered later had originally been the workhouse. Needless to say, it left no impression on me at the time, but when it was pointed out to me on various occasions by my mother that it was where I was born, it seemed to have a cosy cottage and domestic scale which must have been pleasant for my parents and those who worked there, and a contrast with present-day mega-factory hospitals. It serves well as sheltered housing today, now called Ditchburn Place.

Like all children growing up in the 1950s there was compulsory cod liver oil, Bisodol for wind, pink calamine lotion for rashes, Friar's balsam for coughs and catarrh, kaolin and morphine for upset stomachs, and sticky yellow linctus for sore throats. Witch Hazel was dabbed onto bruises and TCP onto cuts. At school we had injections (much feared) against typhoid, polio and smallpox. We were encouraged to get chickenpox, and endure the week-long purgatory of itching, because it was thought safer to have it young rather than get it or the dreaded shingles later in life. Mumps and scarlet fever were definitely to be avoided.

Our family doctor was Tom Anderson who practiced from Rolleston House, his large Edwardian mansion at No.1 Huntingdon Road, opposite the old Murkett's garage at the junction with Victoria Road and Histon Road. He was a tall imposing man, with enormous ears and a booming voice of great authority and command. He was slightly younger than my parents, who thought he was marvellous, and although I was a little scared of him, I liked him too. He had a genial manner and was normally dressed in baggy corduroy trousers and a tweed jacket with leather elbow patches, stethoscope around his neck. He was very keen on sport, being an eminent oarsman and coach, with his oar from his boat race blue prominently displayed in the surgery waiting room. In his spare time he could frequently be seen on the river towpath, bawling instructions and encouragement to a college crew. He knew I was mad about cricket and rugby, and he always had kind words for me.

His colleague or partner (I never really knew) was far more formidable. Dr Alice Roughton was an eccentric, driving a battered old American soft-topped jeep with open sides, and later a Mini Moke. She was also a keen pilot. Whenever she came to our house with someone, usually me, ill in bed, she would storm in and regardless of the time of year or temperature outside proceed to fling open all the windows. 'Fresh air, fresh air!' she would exclaim, 'That's all you need'. I'm sure she was excellent in her diagnoses and prescriptions, but I don't remember her saying anything else. My mother was scared of her too.

The third and most junior member of the practice was Dr Duncan Ballantine, gentle, softly-spoken and immensely sympathetic. We all liked him.

After long bouts of sickness and stomach pains when, confined to bed, I would listen to the Light Programme and yearn for Russ Conway or Mrs Mills on the piano, it was eventually decided that there was something radically wrong, and I was referred to Addenbrooke's Hosptial Outpatients for tests.

In the 1950s Addenbrooke's was still entirely on its original site fronting onto Trumpington Street, hard to believe now that the modern Addenbrooke's at Hills Road occupies vast acreages and is one of the largest hospitals in Europe. When I was just four, my father had been in the Ear, Nose and Throat ward for an operation to remove some blockage in his nose, after which he had to give up his pipe, so I'd visited the inside before. In any event, Addenbrooke's was a familiar landmark, close to our church, also on Trumpington Street.

The outpatients had its own entrance straight onto the road, now occupied by Browns Restaurant. It was not a very friendly or welcoming place. The hard surfaces of the polished terrazzo floors and tiled walls reflected every sound, magnifying them into a cacophony of echoes. Above all, the smell of ether, formaldehyde or disinfectant permeated the air and the fabric. My mother and I seemed to spend interminable hours in the waiting room. When we were summoned to a cubicle a nurse would brusquely swish round some curtains for privacy and I was then subjected to a succession of examinations, urine samples, and worse, having strange instruments and tubes inserted up my bottom, being made to drink oddly coloured liquids, and all sorts of other indignities.

The only redeeming thing was Mr Withercombe. He was the specialist who eventually decided after several visits that I had a defective kidney and that it had to be removed. He was a mild-mannered, petite, inscrutable gentleman. He seemed entirely trustworthy, and unquestionably competent. I couldn't understand at the time why he was called 'Mister', rather than 'Doctor'. It still seems strange that surgeons are given the distinction of being so addressed.

Thus, aged seven, I was admitted to Addenbrooke's Hospital to have my dud kidney removed. Those were not the days of keyhole surgery, nor were such operations routine. I remember being worried about the size of the cut they would need to make, and my mother reassuringly saying it would just be a tiny scratch. As it turned out they opened me up from belly-button to backbone, and I still have the scar to prove it.

The Childrens' Ward was on the third floor of the north wing and my bed overlooked the front courtyard, which at that time was a huge tarmac car park, devoid of any planting. It became a very familiar and welcome view. Mr Withercombe was clearly a 'star' and did an excellent job, setting me on a healthy course. Having been admitted in February I was allowed home in April, and my parents came to collect me in the car.

When we got home it was 6 p.m. and still light. The birds were singing, and the garden was full of the greenery of spring. I ran out of the veranda doors and onto the lawn under the apple trees, still wet from a shower of rain, and the air as fresh as it has ever felt in my nostrils.

Apart from visits to the Outpatients to have my stitches removed and a few check-ups with Dr Janet Roscoe, I never went inside Old Addenbrooke's again. But I felt sad when it closed. Thank goodness it wasn't pulled down, but having lain empty from 1976, it was jazzed up in 1995 by the architect John Outram and put to good use as the Judge Business School.

New Addenbrooke's always felt soulless in comparison. It began to emerge in the 1960s, on the arable fields south of Long Road where on wintry Wednesday mornings we'd been sent on cross-country runs from school. The tall boiler house chimney was an early landmark, or blot on the landscape as many people said. When my father had the first of his heart problems in the 1970s, it was New Addenbrooke's that we visited, never a joyful experience. When he had a bypass operation in the 1980s, it took place in the specialist Papworth Hospital which was altogether a more charming place, quite rural in its situation as befitted a former isolation and TB clinic. The old buildings at Papworth had character, with high ceilings and chimney-breasts, and the gardens outside were a delight, full of snowdrops and bluebells, as I pushed my father along the gravel paths in his wheel chair. Such things surely help an optimistic patient. It certainly gave my father a new, if brief, lease of life.

Our dentist was Mr Betts whose premises, Gregory & Betts Dental Surgery, were on the corner of Glisson Road and Gresham Road, very close to Fenner's cricket ground. He was an affable, chuckling silver-haired man with a broad face and a wide if thin smile. He always seemed genial to me, but perhaps that's because I had good teeth and never had to undergo any unpleasant treatment. When I was nine or ten I did have to wear a brace to push out my upper teeth but that didn't involve any injections or the dreaded gas. My brother, who had bad teeth, hated him, and my father didn't trust him either. He continued to go to a dentist in Bedford whom he'd first been to before the war. I liked Mr Betts because his waiting room had more interesting magazines than the doctors or Addenbrooke's, and the pink mouthwash seemed delicious.

Rather reassuringly No. 45 Glisson Road is still a dentist today, the Oasis Dental Clinic, maybe not so surprising given that planning permission is hard to come by for such uses in residential streets, and thus not lightly relinquished.

## SCHOOL PART II

My foray into the privileged world of private, or at least Direct Grant, schooling at the Perse Prep was a brief one. My brother before me had gone into the state secondary system, and so did I. In September 1962, having presumably passed the eleven-plus, I followed my brother and started at the Cambridgeshire High School for Boys, or the County as it was commonly known. Without a scolarship I doubt whether the senior Perse was an option financially for my parents. They had only been able to afford the Prep because Roger had left before I started. In any case the County was reckoned to be just as good, if not better.

In the 1960s Cambridge still had a selective and single-sex secondary school system. In the private, or perversely called 'public' sector, there was the Leys School on Trumpington Road, boys only and mainly boarders, and the Perse, with separate boys and girls schools on Hills Road and Panton Street. The Perse was academically better than the Leys and had subsidised fees, being a Direct Grant school, and a tiny number of scholarships. The new Perse boys school by Robert Matthew, Johnson Marshall architects, was also much admired. I had had the privilege of presenting Princess Alexandra with a bouquet of flowers at the opening ceremony in 1958.

In the state system there were the two High Schools, boys and girls, which were available after eleven-plus selection to children from the whole of Cambridgeshire, and two grammar schools, the girls in Victorian premises on Parkside, and the boys in a brand new building in Queen Edith's Way. The grammars were definitely a rung down from the high schools, and seemed to take children only from within the city. Rather naively as a child, when I heard adults talking about or criticising the 'grammar school' system, I assumed they were discussing the grammar schools peculiar to Cambridge. In reality the High School was just as much a grammar school too.

As well as the grammars, there were the secondary moderns, like the Manor and Netherhall, and the 'tech' (Cambridge College of Arts and Technology) which offered post-sixteen education for those who couldn't get into or weren't cut out for a school sixth-form.

The County Boys' school occupied a good-sized site on Hills Road, on the right-hand side after crossing the railway bridge as one goes out of town. Between the school and the bridge was a small parade of local shops, and King and Harpers' garage was opposite, on the corner with Cherry Hinton Road. The main frontage building was an imposing three-storey Edwardian structure, purpose-built in 1903 in a vaguely neo-Tudor style, but given splayed bay additions in 1924 when the north and south wings were also added. In 1958 a new single-storey gymnasium and changing rooms and a two-storey science block were added behind the school hall and the south wing, thus forming a western side to the quadrangle which was the main supervised tarmac playground of the school. Behind and south of the hall, where the theatre was eventually

CAMBRIDGESHIRE HIGH SCHOOL  FOR BOYS JULY 1966

School photograph, 1966. (Ray Studies Ltd)

built, and to the west of the gym and chemistry labs, were the 'huts'. These were extraordinary structures, apparently put up in 1922 to last for fifteen years, but which were to endure for fifty (one even until 2009). They were made of timber studs with chicken wire, pebble-dashed on the outside and clad with timber boards inside, with corrugated asbestos roofs, painted concrete floors and rusting Crittall windows. We froze in winter, roasted in summer. During the 1960s there were false promises of new buildings and improvements, and they never happened. The teaching staff felt frustrated and jealous of the Perse and Grammar boys' schools, even the County Girls on Long Road which had been built in 1938 to a very high standard.

Around the huts and beyond were extensive playgrounds, part tarmac, part grass, an area known as the orchard, plus the big field on the other side of Purbeck Road which was the dead-end lane leading to Rattee and Kett's builder's yard. We were lucky to have such a generous expanse for informal play. On top of that was the proper sports field, ten minutes walk away in Luard Road, fronting on to the railway lines. This was big enough for several rugby pitches, cricket pitches and tennis courts, and boasted a satisfyingly symmetric pavilion whose concrete walls and floors echoed with the sound of boot studs and energetic voices.

Having been a medium-sized fish in the tiny pond of prep school, I was now a minnow in a bigger sea. The County had about 600 boys, about thirty-five teachers, and was a three-form entry with ninety-six pupils in my first year. These three forms were maintained up to the fifth or O-Level year, but then the sixth-form was smaller, with only fifty per year.

For the first year we were arranged alphabetically into our classes, which were called 2WG, 2WL and 2RW, being the initials of the form masters, Gumbrell, Lowey and Watson. It was odd that the first year was called the second form. The fourth year was called the 'Removes', so that year five got back on track and was properly called the fifth-form. I never heard a sensible or logical explanation for this.

At the end of the first-year tests there was streaming into A, B, and C classes and this segregation remained right through to O-levels. In the A stream Latin was compulsory, because it was a prerequisite for an Oxbridge place, and unquestionably the main academic objective of the school was to maximise university entry. The limited number of teachers and the large class sizes meant there were other even more bizarre choices of subjects. At the end of the second year we had to choose between history and geography, and could only take one of these at O-Level. Having been bored to death by Mr Watson who droned on and on about Samian pottery, and frightened to death by 'Whacker' Warne, Geography was the easy and obvious choice for me. We then had to choose between Physics and Biology (again an easy choice because my brother had excelled at physics and I wanted to be different), and finally to opt for one of Chemistry, German or Greek, where the affable 'Doc' Adamson got my vote. After the first year we even had to drop either art or woodwork. Again the decision was influenced by the charisma of the teacher, so the twinkling eyes and skilful chisel of the elfin and bearded Mr Pendred easily won the day over the crusty and critical Mr Harden. Sadly in the zeal for traditional grammar school education, the arts took a back seat and were regarded as a hobby rather a serious subject. I had to do my O- and A-Level Music exams outside school. Inside school Denis Fielder, the music teacher, did his best on zero-resources, but his great influence on me was beyond the classroom.

In the small sixth-form there was a complete separation of arts and science, and no opportunity to mix. Subjects such as Philosophy, Media Studies, Politics and Current Affairs did not exist then in the school curriculum. From a current perspective these limitations might seem like drawbacks, and no doubt they were part of the emerging debate about comprehensive schools, bigger buildings and greater opportunities. At the time you just got on with it.

Tom Marsden. (*The Cantabrigian*, 1968, G.P. Pawelec)

After the surrogate-mother lady teachers at Milton Road and the Perse Prep, the County was, at least to begin with, an all-male world. Among the teachers, whose ages ranged from twenty-five to sixty-five, there was a vast range of potential role-models to admire or ogres and villains to dislike.

I was lucky enough in my first year to catch the last full year of Peter Layng who had started teaching at the County in 1924. Unsurprisingly known as 'Grandad', his avuncular and patient manner was a great comfort, and there was surely sadness in his voice as he meticulously recited his Latin declensions to us, eyes half raised to the ceiling. Mr Layng had been the deputy head, and was replaced by George Barlow, who developed a similarly humane and benevolent role. Such was the universal respect that his nickname was nothing crueller than 'George'. Such a disposition was in part a necessary balance to the Head, A. W. Eagling, from whom most pupils kept a wary distance. He did teach a bit of Latin, but not to me, and apparently spoke excellent Italian. To most of us he was a disciplinarian, with a booming voice of imperious authority and a laugh akin to Brian Blessed. He abhorred litter, and on his rounds was often heard barking 'Small boy, pick up that piece of paper!' He always wore his black gown, even when riding his bicycle, and with his round face and owl-like features he was commonly known as 'The Beak'.

Other nicknames for teachers were ruder or more infantile. The Lancastrian Harry Eckersley, one-time PE teacher but diverted by injury and age to General Studies, was still known as 'Rubber guts'. Peter Bilton, the young Biology assistant who cocked his head on one side, was more wittily known as 'Isaiah', because one eye was higher than the other. 'Gummy', 'Snoz', 'Piggy', 'Satch' and 'Taffy' were more prosaic names, and rather unkind. They deserved better, and with due respect I have not appended their surnames. Those who remember will know!

I too had my nickname. In my class there were ten Johns and eleven Roberts. I was the only Alec in the entire school, such are the changing fashions of names. However, aged eleven, individuality is not a comfort, whereas conformity is everything. In the absence of a William in my class I was renamed 'Bill'. It was a private name, just among my mates. Most teachers didn't know and my parents had no inkling. It persisted for seven years at school, and then was instantly shed.

Despite their mannerisms several teachers provided inspiration or the spark of understanding and enlightenment. Tom Marsden, called 'Plug' because of his hearing-aid, was a brilliant Maths teacher who in his jovial Yorkshire way had the gift of clear explanation. He and his wife sang in our church choir, and in the Cambridge Philharmonic chorus with my mother, and perhaps paid special attention to my brother and I. Mr Bols (unfortunately 'Slob' backwards) was the opposite. His supposedly simple 'caveman' methods, where he would painstakingly write out multiplications in the form of addition, drove us mad. He was soon moved to another school, and replaced by the equally unfortunately named Dr Dobbie.

The mix of control, liberty and mutual respect varied enormously between pupils and different teachers. Thirty boys in a class have a cruel knack for exposing weakness. The mass-banging of desk lids, the hiding of chalk and the turning-round of desks before the onset of a lesson were all inflicted on the unwary. Poor Monsieur Chezot, the volatile French 'assistante', was even goaded into shattering a window with a misguided blackboard rubber.

Johnny Walker, who lived next door to our friends the Allansons when they moved to Pound Close in Bottisham, was a radical, impulsive and very popular head of English. As well as making us read and act Shakespeare in class he brought Chaucer alive, made Dickens approachable, Swift understandable, and introduced us to twentieth-century figures such as Auden, Dylan Thomas and Wilfred Owen. Johnny Walker and the new Classics master, Roger Dalliday, directed ambitious school plays, such as Aristotle's *The Birds*, Ionesco's *Rhinoceros*, Brecht's *Caucasian Chalk Circle* and Goldoni's *The Servant of Two Masters*. These were staged in the main hall, but involved collaboration with the Girls County and the Perse Girls. There was keen competition to participate, and fortunately for me they usually included music. Even my brother got involved with the lighting for the production of Beckett's *Waiting for Godot*.

The methodical and sensible Peter Bryan was in charge of Geography and set me on a course which was to guide much of my later life. He was both encouraging and demanding, with a keen eye for the particular abilities and requirements of different individuals in his class. The field trips at the end of the Easter holidays were memorable, even though we had incessant drizzle in Hindhead, snow in Whitby and driving rain in Dawlish. Thirty boys in a coach, driven by the admirable Reg, and staying in youth hostels made for some unruliness but a lot of fun, and helped spark a genuine interest in the wider environment, plus an initiation in the delights and dangers of alcohol.

In my fourth year, in April 1966, I went with Mr Lowey's French party to Paris, my first excursion abroad. We travelled by train and ferry, stayed in the Hotel Metropole, a rather drab establishment in Boulevard de Magenta near the Place de la Republique, and spent five exhausting days tramping the streets and seeing the sights. The whole trip, paid for in instalments by my parents, cost £28. I don't think it helped my French much.

That same summer I went on the army camp to the Brecon Beacons. The Combined Cadet Force had been a major and compulsory part of school life in the 1950s and early '60s unless you were in the Scouts. I caught the end of it. For some reason I chose the army section, maybe because the RAF spent all their time messing around with a grounded glider and a large rubber band, and the navy section were preoccupied with flags and knots. The army was probably worse. The khaki uniform and beret, worn all day every Wednesday, was unbearably itchy and the boots and spats were heavy and uncomfortable. Endless hours were spent square-bashing, being shouted at, or cleaning rifles. Occasionally we went to the rifle range on Barton Road and struggled to load and fire the unwieldy Lee Enfield 303s (probably First World War surplus). Extraordinarily even in 1966 the targets were still cardboard cut-outs of German soldiers, complete with square jaws and Nazi helmets. We took turns in holding up the dummies from behind the bunker and sent mischievously misleading information back to those who were firing, so that even a bulls-eye would be told 'aim left', 'more left', and so on until they were shooting at the next target.

At the summer camp we had to do a night exercise, with blackened faces, armed with blanks and flares, and stumbled around featureless expanses of moorland and bog. On one sortie our lorry skidded off the road and we all ended up in a ditch, somewhat shaken. We slept, or didn't sleep, in bleak Nissen huts on camp beds under coarse blankets, but we did all manage to cram into the NAAFI mess to watch the World Cup Final. The cheering was long and loud.

The CCF was run by several of the teachers who had done military service and liked to inflict discipline on their pupils. Yet despite all the huff and puff of Lieutenant-Colonel Perkins, Major Hyde, Captain Foster, Lieutenant Mantell (RNR) and Flight-Lieutenant Watson, it was our humble school caretaker, Mr Wagstaff, who took the salute during the annual inspection. He had been a squadron leader in the war and out-ranked them all. In 1967 the CCF was phased out, much to my relief, and replaced with community service, which involved gardening for old age pensioners at Abbeyfield Homes or washing WVS meals-on-wheels vans.

The 1960s were a time of immense social change and new waves of popular culture, all of which brushed uneasily against a traditional grammar school. The symbolic zenith of the High School's achievements and respectability was, perhaps, winning the BBC Radio Top of the Form in the autumn 1963. The whole school had packed into the hall for each round, wildly clapping each victory. When, to the question 'What is Liverpool famous for?' Paul Richens answered 'the Beatles', it even earned a slot on Pick of the Week.

The tight regulations on school uniforms were gradually relaxed. When I started in 1962, the wearing of caps and ties outside school had been compulsory, but difficult to enforce. All boy wore shorts until they were fourteen or fifteen, and because my mother expected me to wear my brother's cast-offs I did the same, although by 1966 I was the only boy in class not to be in long-trousers, and much ragged for it. Fortunately I was small, rather than a bean-pole, so perhaps did not look quite so ridiculous. By the time I reached the sixth-form and became a prefect, we were allowed to wear jackets of our choice, not school blazers. Teachers too by then had abandoned their gowns.

Lapses of discipline were punished by detention, otherwise known as 'clink'. For the worst misdemeanours there was Saturday morning detention where, under the stern direction of Mr Wagstaff (who we called the 'General'), you had to sweep the playground and clean the bike sheds. Prefects dished out a form of lines, or 'pensum', which was a tediously long recitation, to be written out as many times as was thought fit. Photocopying was not an option in those days. There are some, including my brother, who can remember to this day the precise wording, 'The Pensum is a reminder that the orderly life of the school can be maintained only by the strict observance of certain rules and regulations, any infringement of which, however insignificant it may appear to the offender, is detrimental to the well-being of the whole community.'

Because my brother was four academic years ahead of me we had not overlapped at the Perse Prep. At the County I had the strange experience of an older sibling at the same school, and all the invidious comparisons from teachers and ribaldry from pupils that inevitably occur. Generally we kept out of each other's way.

Only one of my contemporaries at the Perse Prep came with me to the County, all the others went on to the senior Perse. That one was John Sharpe, who hadn't been exactly a bosom-pal but who now for a couple of years became a good chum. His father, Dr (later Professor) Alan Sharpe was an academic and don at Jesus College, and they lived in a college house, No. 1 Claremont, which was a small courtyard of two Victorian terraces off Hills Road, five minutes walk closer into town. Before I was allowed to cycle on my own to school their house became a useful refuge for me after school finished before getting a lift home with my father from his office in Brooklands Avenue. It was John and his father who introduced me to the boyish pleasures of train-spotting. John also had an enviable Hornby oo gauge electric train layout, with lots of complicated points and tracks and masses of engines and rolling stock. For an eleven-year-old, it was a good place to spend an hour and a half. Coincidentally this same house, owned by Jesus College, was later lived in by Nick and Judith Shackleton and Christopher Hogwood, and visited by me in very different circumstances.

I quickly lost touch with my old playground friends from the Perse Prep, even John Tebbit and Charles Wellington. Like most little boys I wasn't good at keeping in contact with people I didn't see every day. At the County there was a bigger choice, a wider range of backgrounds, poorer and better off. In the playground I was drawn to those who listened to the same radio programmes, being a complete outsider to any discussion of television soaps such as Z-Cars or Top of the Pops. Fortunately there were enough of us who were addicted to 'Round The Horne', and mimicking the nonsense of 'Rambling Syd Rumpo', 'J. Peasemold Gruntfuttock' and 'Julian and Sandy'. Otherwise breaktime involved multi-sided anarchic bouts of football and more disciplined games of 'spot', where a rebounding ball was kicked in sequence against a 'goal' chalked on a wall. Quite rarely there was a punch-up, and a crowd would gather round the combatants, chanting 'fight, fight, fight…' until a master or prefect intervened. Smokers hid round the back of the bike sheds or in the bushes on Purbeck Road. Rather than endure the rota and stench of canteen dinners I took sandwiches, made by my long-suffering mother.

Over seven years at the same school I learnt that different people develop at different speeds, and one's friendships shifted. Philip Augar, who had been in the bottom stream from the start, got eight O-Levels, followed by three 'A's at A-Level and went on to read History at Clare. As the author of *The Death of Gentlemanly Capitalism* and *The Greed Merchants*, he has perhaps been the highest flier of all my contemporaries. Other subsequently successful old boys before me such as Martin Amis, Tony Palmer, Roger Waters and Roger (Syd) Barrett (founders of Pink Floyd, together with Dave Gilmour who was at the Perse) also hid their lights under barrels at school. By contrast it was no surprise that Jacko Page went on to play rugby for Cambridge University and England, or that (Sir) Kevin Tebbit would end up as a top civil servant.

Once in the sixth-form, I too became a prefect, and enjoyed the privileges, especially the table tennis table, of the prefects' common room. Simon Tulitt, who lived in Abington, became my best pal, so much so that after finishing A-levels in June 1969 the two of us went to Iceland on a Henry Morris Travel Bursary, provided by the Education Authority.

In the late '60s all the talk was about co-education and the new comprehensive system, abolishing the eleven-plus and getting rid of streaming. In 1965 we had a new Maths teacher, Mrs Gent, but apart from the cleaners and dinner ladies she was the only female in the school. School Speech Days, held in the Guildhall, were occasions for visiting dignitaries to air their views about the future of the school. Most of them were Masters of Cambridge colleges, such as Lord Todd, Sir Eric Ashby and Owen Chadwick. I imagine that they were chosen for their sympathetic attitudes. Shirley Williams would not have been the first choice. In 1967, collecting a prize, I shook the limp and clammy hand of Lord (Rab) Butler, Master of Trinity College, one-time Chancellor of the Exchequer, Home Secretary , Foreign Secretary, and major contributor to the 1944 Education Act. As a true-blue Tory he spoke out against change, and received great applause, but the writing, as decreed by the Labour Government in 1965, was on the wall.

In 1968 Mr Eagling retired as headmaster and was replaced by Colin Hill, who clearly had his eye on a different future. Several other new young teachers were also keen on change. That came just too late for me. In 1971 Sir David Robinson, old boy and owner of Robinson TV rentals, paid for the construction of a new theatre. In 1972 the final decision was taken by the

THE CANTABRIGIAN

As Proposed by the Education Committee :

**FOR SALE**

as surplus to Comprehensive Requirements
The distinguished Scholastic Establishment

known as

**THE CAMBRIDGESHIRE HIGH SCHOOL FOR BOYS**

This Gentleman's Estate of great historical and educational interest, with Extensive Grounds containing Mature Timber and Distinctive Outbuildings, is to be offered either as a whole or in Lots, viz :

Lot 1 : Comprising the Mayne Building, including Class-rooms with choice decor in Off-white, biology labs. and sixth-form accommodation in genuine antique condition, with Staff Room for 35 teachers (standing room only), and Cellarage for sandwich-eaters and troglodyte chess-players.

Lot 2 : Comprising the Hall, genuine 1933 renovated 1956, scene of many Dramatic Performances, moving Religious Services, and renowned victories over G.C.E. Examiners ; moral inscriptions illustrate the building's long and distinguished academic associations.

Lot 3 : Comprising separate wing known as 'The Huts' circa 1920, containing a wealth of oak beams. Ideal for conversion to Infant School, as the roof does not leak.

Lot 4 : Comprising the 'New Wing', containing up-to-date Gym and Laboratories, added ten years ago as part of a Rebuilding Project which the Education Committee failed to complete.

Lot 5 : Comprising various buildings on the Estate, some with Vacant Possession, including 3-bedroomed Lodge, Greenhouse, Rabbit Farm and usual offices.

The development of this important site would keep any Planning Dept. busy for at least 50 years.

To be offered for sale by Public Auction (unless saved by Private Treaty)

**at the Shire Hall in 1975**

by Messrs.

**≫FEBRUARY'S≪**

*The School for sale*
*— see page 24*

Front cover of *The Cantabrigian*, 1967.

Education Authority that the Cambridgeshire High School for Boys should become the new sixth-form college for Cambridge. In September 1974 that came to pass. Unwittingly I had been virtually at the end of an era, one of the last intake to sail uninterrupted through the seven years of a state grammar school in Cambridge.

They say that your school days are the best days of your life. I don't go with that. For me the pressure-cooker of secondary school did not promote a carefree or self-determined existence. On reflection I was glad that I went to a comparatively small school where teachers knew the names of all the pupils, and vice versa. There were benefits too in having an integrated sixth-form rather than having to leave for a separate sixth-form college. I did well in the established system of syllabuses and exams, as opposed to the current fad for flexibility and continuous assessment, and did not rebel against the dragooning discipline of selection and streaming, but when the time came I was happy to leave. I was relieved that I didn't have to do a third year in the sixth-form. When I passed out of the school gates for the last time, sometime in June 1969, I did so with no feeling of regret or sentiment. It was time to move on.

## *HOLIDAYS*

My father had three weeks' annual holiday, which was the going rate for an office job in the austere 1950s. Only when he was promoted from 'engineer' to 'senior engineer' in 1964 was his allowance increased to four weeks. Two of those weeks were taken for a family holiday every August. The rest were used for doing DIY jobs at home, decorating the house or a short excursion around the Bank Holidays at Easter or Whitsun.

For many years we went to the same place on the west coast of Wales, south of Aberystwyth and Aberaeron on Cardigan Bay. Aberporth was never a particularly pretty place, even less

Ceridfa, Aberporth with Mrs Griffiths, August 1963. (Author's Collection)

so today as bungalows have sprawled across the headlands, but was a very practical base for a seaside holiday.

We stayed in a spacious 1920s house called 'Ceridfa' where Mrs Griffiths dispensed bed, breakfast and evening meals. The house had a generous hallway and a baronial staircase with a long stained-glass window running past the half landing. There were three guest bedrooms, and usually there were five of us, either grandmother 'Ga' or a school friend of mine or my brother.

It was a short walk down the hill to the big sandy beach. A little brook ran down the right-hand side, perfect for damming and diverting, and there were conveniently sculpted rocks to sit on, all washed clean by the tide leaving countless rock pools to explore.

On the west headland of the small north-facing bay was a Ministry of Defence rocket testing site. August was normally their holiday period, but once amid great excitement Mrs Griffiths announced at breakfast that today there was to be a launch at 11.00 a.m. Sure enough, we were among a small gathering assembled on the little grass strip on the east headland to witness the puff of white smoke, an echoing boom and a vapour trail as the projectile streaked out to sea.

Mrs Griffiths was tiny, her greying black hair tightly clamped inside a hair net, and always dressed in a floral apron. She spoke Welsh, and taught us a few phrases such as *boreda* and *mi brekfast yn barod*. She was also avidly 'green', composting everything possible, burning anything combustible on her stove, and even flattening tin cans with a hammer so they could be collected, once a year. More amusingly, most evenings she engaged in extraordinarily long telephone conversations in Welsh to her friends where the stream of incomprehensible jabbering was broken by the occasional 'tellywelly' or 'twenty cigarettes' for which presumably there was no Welsh equivalent.

Often we walked along the cliff-top to the next bay at Tresaith. This was a pleasant path lined with foxgloves, bracken, sea pink and gorse and with scary vertical drops to inaccessible coves below on one side, and fields of ripening corn sweeping inland on the other. Perched near the cliff-edge were a couple of old railway carriages converted into little dwellings, and we wondered how on earth they had been transported there, given that the nearest railway was miles away. Sadly today these charming shacks have spawned a rash of mobile, or rather, immobile homes all the way to Tresaith, even above the spectacular waterfall which cascades onto the rocks beside the beach.

My favourite place was Llangranog which was a short drive from Aberporth. This was an altogether prettier spot, the village squeezed into a steep narrow valley whose sides were covered with stunted, wind-swept trees. In front of the parking-lot a river fanned out across a stony foreshore, but around the corner from the weirdly photogenic rock outcrop was the most perfect sandy beach you could ever find.

When it rained, as it sometimes did, we went to one of the nearby towns. New Quay had a busy fishing harbour whereas Cardigan, or Aberteifi as it is now know, seemed very dull. In the 1950s and '60s place names and road markings were not bilingual; *ARAF* was not painted everywhere on the tarmac. Most frequently we would go to Newcastle Emlyn and having parked in the cattle market, we'd mooch up and down the main street in our plastic macks or anoraks, and perhaps pay a visit to the Teifi Tearooms. Opposite the Pelican Inn was Jenkins Butchers where my mother would buy cold meats or pork pie for our picnic lunch, consumed inside our steamed-up car if the rain was incessant. Downstream from Newcastle Emlyn on the River Teifi was Cenarth with its waterfalls, rapids and watermill, and a wide, stone road-bridge punctured with circular holes to allow flood water to pass. We would walk along the smooth and slippery rocky path on the wooded banks of the river, or if we were lucky, watch the coracle men in their archaic craft skilfully stretching their salmon nets across the turbulent flow between two of their little round boats.

In many ways the most memorable part of the Welsh holidays was the journey there and back. My father persuaded me to relieve the tedium of being stuck in the back seat of the car by keeping a logbook of the places we passed through, with the mileage, times and average speeds. The *I-Spy* books were also a useful amusement, collecting points for humped-backed bridges or market crosses. What did impress however were the honey-coloured stone Cotswold cottages, the magical names of the villages such as the Tews, the Swells and the Slaughters, the

River Teifi at Cenarth, August 1962. (Author's Collection)

Coracles on the River Teifi at Cenarth, 1961. (Author's Collection)

palatial Bliss Valley woollen mill outside Chipping Norton, the smooth hump-backed Malvern Hills, the cosy Herefordshire farms with their straggly cider apple trees, the white and black half-timbered houses and precariously jettied upper floors of the inns of Tewkesbury, Ledbury, Leominster and Pembridge, the wild heather moors between Rhayader and Devil's Bridge and the gushing headwaters of the River Wye. These strong recollections were the undoubted benefit of going to the same place year after year.

Three or four times we went to Scotland instead of Wales. My father's mother, who had died when I was very young, was a Macdonald, so there were some Scottish roots. This was a longer drive from Cambridge, too far for a single day, and we broke our journey by stopping overnight in Corbridge, near Hadrian's Wall. Here we always stayed with Mrs Moffat, an elderly lady who ran a higgledy-piggledy guest house very close to the old bridge over the Tyne. She had a telephone with separate ear and mouth pieces, a grandfather clock with an astonishingly loud tick and she offered us black pudding to go with our poached eggs for breakfast.

Our destination on the second day was Auntie Janet's sturdy house beside the Clyde at Craigendoran Avenue, on the outskirts of Helensburgh. From her front door it was brief scamper to the sea wall and the little low-tide beach with its patches of sand and big smooth rocks slimy with seaweed, and heady with the tangy smell of salt water and fish. In the 1950s and early '60s Craigendoran pier was a thriving hive of activity, and still the home base and overnight berth of the wonderful quartet of Clyde paddle-steamers, the *Waverley*, the *Talisman*, the *Caledonia* and the *Jeanie Deans*. These boats, together with the *Maids* and *Duchesses* which made up the rest of the Clyde fleet, were the life-blood of our Scottish holidays, and most days we would take a trip of one of the numerous steamer trips on offer. My father and mother would peruse the timetables at the dining table in the evening with Auntie Janet purring encouragingly alongside, planning the next day's adventure. Packed lunches of soft floury baps filled with potted meat or processed cheese, tomatoes and chunks of cucumber, apples, orange squash and a thermos of tea would be prepared.

Those trips left strong memories. The distinctive thrash of the paddles churning through the water, the freshly scrubbed timber decks and seats, the gleamingly polished pistons and brass in

On the Clyde with the *Jeanie Deans*, 1964. (Author's Collection)

the engine room below, the swept-back funnels, and the gulls following in the wake; was there ever a more enchanting or romantic way to travel? Almost invariably we would first cross over to Gourock or Greenock for a first port of call, but thereafter the options were many. Between Kilcreggan and Dunoon there were tantalising glimpses into Holy Loch and the mysteriously secret American submarine base. Then it would be on to Innellan with its smart sandstone villas, built before the First World War as retreats for magnates of Glaswegian industry and then perhaps via Wemyss Bay and Largs to Millport on the island of Cumbrae. Often we called in to Rothesay on the island of Bute, with its picture-postcard sea front and tall church steeple. Most exciting was the passage through the narrows of the Kyles of Bute where the rocky land came close on either side, calling in at Tighnabruaich or Auchenlochan on our way to Tarbert on the Mull of Kintyre. Once we took the long trip to Brodick on the Isle of Arran, and a close-up view of Goat Fell. When we returned to Craigendoran the sun had set and the lights of Helensburgh and Greenock were twinkling across the water.

At the time I did not appreciate that the heyday of the Clyde steamers was not only waning but in terminal decline. Within a few years many of the old boats were withdrawn from service. Our last family holiday on Clydeside was in 1964, and that August we unknowingly enjoyed the swan-song of the *Jeanie Deans* and the *Duchess of Montrose*, both laid up after that summer and later scrapped. The *Talisman* was withdrawn in 1966, the *Caledonia* in 1969 and the *Waverley* in 1973. The *Caledonia* became a floating Thames-side restaurant until it was burnt out in 1980 and replaced on the Embankment by the *Queen Mary II*. The *Maids of Argyll, Ashton, Cumbrae* and *Skelmorlie* were all laid off between 1971 and 1973.

Craigendoran was also perfectly located for catching the West Highland Railway for day trips to Fort William or Oban. Once again, these were romantic and exciting journeys, with steam engines pulling and pushing, the observation carriage at the rear, and the exotic names of the tiny halts where we stopped – Ardlui, Crianlarich, Tyndrum and Rannoch. One time we stayed in a guest house in Oban, near McCaig's Folly, so that we could take the ferry to Iona and Fingal's Cave. This was on the finest steamer of them all, the *King George V*, which was withdrawn from service in 1974. There were tears in my father's eyes when he read about it in the newspaper.

There were tears in my eyes when just a year ago I revisited Craigendoran and saw the skeletal remains of the pier, abandoned since 1972, and the rusting railway tracks covered in weeds.

It was said at the time that the increase in people taking foreign holidays made the Clyde steamers unviable. Today it seems a feeble excuse, particularly when one sees how the good burghers of Dresden have managed to salvage and keep going nine of the fabulous pre-war paddle steamers on the River Elbe. Four historic paddle boats on the Clyde today would probably do wonders for the tourist industry and the local economy.

My Uncle John usually spent the summer season at Pitlochry, where his versatile Scottish accents assured him a role in the Festival Theatre company. Pitlochry was a long drive from Helensburgh for a day trip, but it was fun to walk up to the dam above the theatre to watch the salmon jump the fish ladder, and to be with John in his kilt among the heather hills he loved. Once we met up with John at Inverary, having driven past the grey hulks of the old battleships and cruisers on Gare Loch. John took us out on a rowing boat on Loch Fyne, where we were surprised by the movement of a large black shiny 'rock' which turned out to be the fin of a basking shark.

For us Scotland was never a seaside holiday destination; there was always Wales for that. On one rare hot day we did swim in Loch Lomond when we had driven past the rhododendrons to where the road ends at Rowardennan, but freezing Scottish lochs generally seemed better for skimming stones than swimming.

With a piece of heather pinned to the bonnet of the car, it was a long and sad drive home to Cambridge. On the way there were the last backwards glimpses of the receding hills, the gradual ironing out of the landscape as the memories of mountains and moors were replaced by the reality of the dull flat fields of Cambridgeshire and the confines of our little house and garden.

## MUSICAL BEGINNINGS

Both my parents were respectable amateur musicians. In her youth my mother had a fine soprano voice with which she won singing prizes and gave recitals. When she came to Cambridge she took to singing in choirs and joined the Philharmonic Society in 1949. My father played the piano and organ, well enough to accompany Richard Tauber in a concert for the Navy in South Africa in 1939. As a child growing up in Wallasey, his own father had told him of the magical Sunday evening soirées at the Goossens household which he had attended before the First World War. There was music in the blood, and music in our house.

The piano lived in the sitting room, a smart upright Murdoch which my parents had bought re-conditioned from Millers. From a young age I enjoyed sitting on my father's lap between his arms as he played hymns or his favourite Schubert pieces. There was also music on the radio, and I took an early shine to the *Ride of the Valkyries* and the opening of the Grieg and Tchaikovsky piano concertos, with their thundering piano chords. I started piano lessons when I was seven with a lady who lived conveniently nearby at No.172 Gilbert Road. A little pale-blue plaque with white letters beside the front door announced Miss R. Welsh, LRAM, Music Teacher. She was sympathetic and patient, with wavy permed blond hair and sensible cardigans. She charged 3s for each lesson, and with monotonous regularity would say 'now I can afford jam on my bread and butter' when I paid her. For all her foibles she set me in the right direction. I liked to practice, unlike my brother, and probably drove him, my parents and the guinea pig mad. At the Perse Prep I was encouraged to take up the recorder and one Saturday I accompanied my father to Millers in Sidney Street to buy my first musical instrument, a shiny varnished wooden descant, price 19s 6d, and worth every penny.

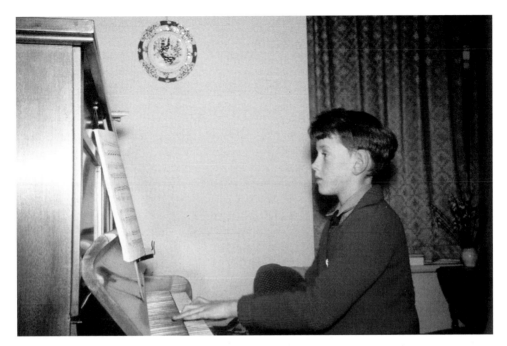

Piano practice, 1962. (Author's Collection)

Miss Carmichael at school and Miss Welsh in Gilbert Road between them sorted out my quavers from my crochets, my minims from my semibreves, and my two-fours from my three-fours. There was no escape from 'Every Good Boy Deserves Favour', 'FACE', and other doggerel acronyms for the order of sharps and flats, but it sunk in. Before long I was moving away from 'Tune A Day' and 'The Farmer's Boy' to Handel's *Largo* and Beethoven's *Minuet in G*.

At some point there was a discussion between Miss Welsh and my mother as to whether I should be put forward for the King's College Choir School as a chorister, but that didn't happen and I was left to tread a more conventional path. Although my parents thought that King's was wonderful I'm not sure that they, as strict non-conformists, would have been comfortable with such a rarefied education for their younger son. Nor indeed might I.

Through singing in the Cambridge Philharmonic Society chorus my mother already regarded its conductor Denis Fielder as a wonderful choir master. By good fortune he was Director of Music at the Cambridgeshire High School and of all the teachers there, he was to have the greatest long-term influence on me.

Denis was slim-faced, slightly built, semi-balding but with his hair over his ears, and wore thick-framed spectacles. He had started teaching at the school in 1946, having been a prisoner of war in the Far East. It was something he never talked about, and he was strongly pacifist and humanist. He was immediately likeable, and was the first grown-up I met who talked to me as if I was an adult, rather than a child.

In my form at the County there were three of us who showed aptitude for playing musical instruments. Michael Cole was a child prodigy, highly strung but a brilliant violinist, pianist and percussionist. He was already composing symphonies, having piano lessons with Denis and aged eleven was given a place in the National Youth Orchestra. John Richens came from a large academic family where everybody played different instruments. Of the older boys, Jonny

Ash played the piano and percussion, and became a good chum. Denis had the good sense to recognise that class music with the rest of the form was not the best use of our time; John and I were allowed to play duets on the grand piano in the main hall instead, and Michael got on with his composing.

One cupboard in the music room contained piles of sheet music, including tattered piano-duet volumes of all the Beethoven and Brahms symphonies, and selected Mozart, Haydn and Schubert. John even found in the Cambridge Music Shop an old arrangement of Mahler's 'Second', where the duettists had to sing as well as play! Fumbling, stumbling or thrashing our way through these dog-eared pages was as good an introduction to these masterpieces as one could wish. For one term only there was a music student doing post-graduate teaching experience at the school. Given his unreasonable expectation that everyone should have perfect pitch, it was just as well that David Atherton pursued a conducting career!

In September 1962 I started having piano lessons from Denis, always after school at his house at No.80 Chesterton Road. There I would first have tea, made by his wife Meg, with whomever of the five children happened to be around, Jill, Hugh, Nick, Andrew and Quetta. The Victorian house was full of unconventional 1960s colours, like pillar-box red and black, with contemporary art and tapestries hanging on the walls, cork tiling on the kitchen floor, exotic rugs on the floor boards; it was another world for me, so different from my own house. The piano lessons were in the big upper-ground floor front room, where the Bechstein grand was piled with scores and long-playing records. Once Titus, the spotty-dog Dalmatian, had been shooed out and the door shut, we would begin. Denis didn't believe in the normal routine of grade exams, with their set pieces, scales and arpeggios. Instead he introduced me to lots of repertoire such as Kabalevsky, Shostakovitch, Debussy's *Preludes*, Dave Brubeck, as well as Bach, Beethoven, Haydn, and Mozart. Of the last he warned me, 'It's easy for children; difficult for adults.' Best of all we played duets, which was the best way to learn to sight-read, particularly as Denis was a marvellous pianist himself. Sometimes he played me pieces on the record player, without showing me the cover, and got me to guess what they might be. Denis lent me books to read and recommended ones to buy or be given for Christmas. It was at Denis' that I was invited to watch the television production of *Billy Budd* in 1966. It was a house I was never in a hurry to leave.

Another cupboard at school contained a small black case with a clarinet inside, and in my second term Denis suggested to me that I might like to play it, so I did. Several older boys at school already played the clarinet and a rather prim lady called Miss Spalding came to the school to give group lessons, which I joined. I must have made good progress. Within a year I had started having individual lessons with John Chapman ,who taught at the Perse Girls, and hired a room for private teaching at the Cambridge Music Shop in All Saints Passage. He was a fantastic clarinettist, who had learnt with the great Frederick Thurston, but he had given up the stress of full-time professional playing and opted for the quieter life of teaching, and living in a little thatched cottage out at Elsworth. With his encouragement, I started playing in the Saturday Morning Orchestra which was run by Geoff Varley, head of music at the Boys Grammar in Queen Ediths Way, and also a fine amateur clarinettist. It was a beginners' orchestra which tackled different pieces each week under Geoff's able baton, making the best of whatever assortment of students turned up, but with a good smattering of Cambridge's peripatetic instrumental teachers.

In April 1964 I attended my first session with the Cambridgeshire Schools Holiday Orchestra. This was a remarkable organisation, founded in 1955 by Molly Gilmour, and which had grown from ten players to over 200. It was directed by the mercurial County Music Advisor, Ludovick Stewart, and through him, funded by the Education Authority. 'Ludo', as he was universally known, was a larger-than-life figure, enthusiastic and expansive in his programming and immensely energetic. Physically he resembled a rather lanky John Barbirolli, although

Bassoon and oboe with John Richens, 1968.
(Author's Collection)

comparisons probably end there. His conducting style was flamboyant, with his wildly flailing baton, his unkempt hair occasionally swept back by his other hand, and his foot stamping on the rostrum to emphasise the beat or to correct a wayward rhythm. Molly was the perfect foil as an administrator, calm and kind, always able to smooth down Ludo's ruffled feathers. She lived in Cory Lodge off Bateman Street which at that time went with her husband's job as Director of the Botanical Gardens.

Ludo was the figurehead, but he relied enormously on the many instrumental teachers who helped individual players, took sectional rehearsals and generally held the whole thing together. Anne Macnaghten, Bernard Blay, Arnold Ashby and David Bass coached the strings, usually about seventy violins, and handful of violas and cellos, and a solitary bass. Geoff Varley looked after the woodwind, aided by Clare Shanks and, for a short while, David Munrow, who tragically committed suicide in 1976. Ted Spratt, who resembled Jimmy Edwards, took the brass and Barry Eaden led the percussion. The rehearsals were held in the main hall of the Girls Grammar on Parkside, where cacophony was slowly turned into symphony, culminating in a grand gala, usually in the Guildhall, all comers welcome. The programmes were both long and ambitious; my first concert comprised Mozart's *Magic Flute Overture,* Beethoven's *Second Symphony,* Vaughan Williams' *Folk Song Suite,* Berlioz's *Symphonie Fantastique,* Sullivan's *Pineapple Poll,* and Rimsky Korsakov's 'March' from the *Coq D'or.* It was not for the faint-hearted.

Among the wind I was one of nineteen clarinets, and one of eight or nine sharing a single music stand, struggling to read some very distant and impossibly hard clarinet part. I soon spotted that there was only one young bassoonist, Ed Warren, alongside the elderly Reuben Stubbings, each with their own separate part and stand.

For all its faults, the Holiday Orchestra was an impressive institution. Somehow I made my way up the ranks and found myself on the coach trips with the smaller selected orchestra to give concerts in Cromer and Linton Village College. The highlight was the exchange with young musicians from Heidelberg, with which Cambridge had been twinned as part of the post-war Anglo-German reconciliation programme. In September 1965 Cambridge hosted a party of young Heidelberg musicians and we put up one of them at home. Christoph Carl was two years older than me, blond, smartly dressed and spoke impeccably polite English. Best of all he played the bassoon, and entranced me with its bright woody sound and clattering keywork. In 1967 we hosted another boy, Karl Michael Krummacher, who was a fine violinist and violist, who went on to become leader of the WDR Rundfunksinfonie orchestra in Cologne.

In 1968 my turn came to visit Heidelberg, a trip that was very nearly cancelled because of the Soviet invasion of Czechoslovakia in August and the fear of hostilities spreading. I was lodged at No.2 Kuno Fischer Strasse with Doctor and Frau Schiffer, he an established lawyer who wore lederhosen and a felt hat, she a quiet housewife who wore a lace bib-apron and heavy tweed skirts. I spoke no German; they had little English but thought I would like beer and boiled eggs for breakfast. There were two concerts in the old castle overlooking the Neckar, conducted by the tyrannical Herr Joachim Kauffmann, who was both physically and temperamentally in the 'screaming skull' mode of George Solti. On the last evening I got to drink my first schnapps, smoke my first cigar, and was sick off the old bridge into the swirling river below.

In October 1965 I got a clarinet of my own, a Besson Bb 'Westminster' (made in the Boosey & Hawkes factory), so that the school instrument could be returned for another beginner. John Chapman, my teacher, helped haggle the price down from 15 guineas to £12. The following autumn I was entered for an audition with the National Youth Orchestra. On a cold grey October day, I caught the train to King's Cross, trudged down Gray's Inn Road to Holborn Library in Theobalds Road, and in an upstairs room nervously played my party piece to Ivey Dickson and Thea King. On the way back to the station the newspaper sellers were shouting the news of the Aberfan disaster. Extraordinarily I was given a place for the Christmas session, and another door was opened in my education.

The NYO had been dormant for a year following the retirement of its founder, Dame Ruth Railton, and its funder, Cecil King, who was her husband. Ivey Dickson was the new director and supervised a fresh intake. On reflection I must have been incredibly lucky. My clarinet playing was no more than moderate; unlike all the others I did not have an A clarinet, only my trusty Bb, so had to transpose. Roger Fallows, the principal clarinet, was very kind to me even though he was three years older and about to go to Cambridge University. I can still hear the effortlessly liquid sound of his solos in Bartok's *Concerto for Orchestra*. I shared a dormitory with Colin Lawson, from Batley, who also played the clarinet, and two Scottish boys, Ian Laing from Buckie and John (Jock) Miller from Fife.

As the tenth of ten clarinets I didn't make the cut for the next National Youth Orchestra session. I carried on with the clarinet, and started playing in some better Cambridge orchestras such as Stephen Bonner's Cambridge Youth Chamber Orchestra and the Cambridge Mozart Orchestra, conducted by Ed Warren, where I played second clarinet alongside Geoff Varley. By then I had even got an A clarinet, bought second hand from George Howarth which had involved a trip to the Aladdin's cave of their premises in Montpelier Grove, Kentish Town, at that time one of the grubbier parts of London. However, when Ed Warren bought his own bassoon before going to study at the Royal College of Music and returned the Holiday Orchestra's instrument I snapped it up. The Warrens lived only a few hundred yards from me in St Albans Way, off Roseford Road, and Ed proved to be an excellent teacher. Even at college he came home most weekends. Such was the shortage of bassoonists in Cambridge that I was playing in orchestras within a few weeks, before I had barely learnt the basic fingering.

In 1968 I got back into the National Youth Orchestra, as a general musician and fledgling bassoonist. I was lucky enough to have composition lessons with Herbert Howells and Alan Richardson, husband of the oboist and wind coach Janet Craxton. Back in Cambridge I started playing in the Uttlesford Orchestra, a chamber ensemble directed by the madly manic George Barker. They rehearsed in his rambling house in Uttlesford and gave concerts in Saffron Walden, Much Hadham, Thaxted and Audley End.

My parents were anxious about what I should do after school, where the choice lay between the two subjects I was good at, Music and Geography.

A work colleague of my father, Henry Moon, happened to share a house with Sir Thomas Armstrong who had been Principal of the Royal College of Music from 1955 and who had just retired in the summer of 1968. On a hot July afternoon I was taken to see him in their beautiful mansion in Newton Blossomville, the other side of Bedford. While Henry Moon amused my father with his collection of vintage racing cars and his device for cutting the lawn with a motor-mower on a rope which wrapped itself around a central post, I had an audience with Sir Thomas. Surprisingly for a music educationalist he advised that I keep music as a hobby, 'If you are clever enough to do something else, then keep music for pleasure'.

My parents also invited Denis Fielder to come round to our house to discuss the matter. Denis agreed with Sir Thomas.

For all his talents as teacher and pianist, Denis Fielder's greatest contribution to Cambridge was his conducting, particularly of choirs. In the 1950s he had started the Combined School Choirs where anyone from the secondary schools was encouraged to join in. From such raw material Denis conjured the highest standards. The elderly Ralph Vaughan Williams even travelled from Surrey to the Cambridge Guildhall in 1954 to hear and applaud the Combined Choir perform his oratorio *The Sons of Light*. With the Cambridge Philharmonic Orchestra and Chorus, which he conducted from 1953 to 1969, Denis also explored a challenging repertoire – Stravinsky, Tippett, Copland, and Kodaly, as well as the normal choral staple-diet of Messiahs and Elijahs.

Denis Fielder surprised everybody in 1968 by announcing his departure, to live and teach in Bishop's Stortford. I felt almost let down that he was leaving before I had finished at school. His last concert with the Phil. was in January 1969 where he shared the conducting duties with Hugh Macdonald, who was to be his successor. Denis played the demanding solo piano part in Constant Lambert's *Rio Grande*, and his great friend Arnold Ashby was the soloist in Elgar's *Cello Concerto*. Denis also conducted the orchestra in the *Concertante for Orchestra with piano* (left hand) by Arnold Bax and asked me to turn the pages for the one-armed pianist Douglas Fox

Denis Fielder conducting in the Guildhall. (Cambridge Newspapers Ltd)

in the concert. Somehow, at the first page turn, the tatty music fell off the stand onto the floor, and I had the indignity of retrieving it on my hands and knees, while Mr Fox ploughed on as if nothing had happened. Of course, he knew it perfectly well from memory!

Denis' departure was the end of an era for Cambridge. His replacement at the High School, Peter Charlton, could hardly have been expected to fill his boots. Indeed, he made me and John Richens take it in turns to play the piano for the hymns in morning assembly, having suffered the indignity of drawing pins placed on the strings by sabateurs.

I did once go to play for Denis at Bishop's Stortford College, playing bassoon in the Fauré *Requiem*, but I didn't keep in touch. In August 2005 I visited him at his home for lunch with Jonny Ash, who had remained friends with his son Hugh. Denis was frail, bowed and thin, with a stick, but still had his high gentle voice and a sparkle in his eye. Titus the Dalmatian had been replaced by Rocky the Greyhound. The same old Bechstein was piled with music and scores. After lunch Denis played *Clair de Lune*, and a medley of Gershwin songs.

Denis died on 19 August 2007. On the following New Years Day, at the end of the final credits of Tony Palmer's film on the life of Vaughan Williams, broadcast on Channel Five, there was a simple dedication; 'to Denis Fielder, school music teacher'.

# SPORT

In his youth, my father had been good at sport. Before the war he had played cricket for the Navy as a wicketkeeper-batsman and rugby for Bedford as a fly-half. His enthusiasm for sport rubbed off on me. We would go to every Saturday game at Grange Road to watch the university rugby team. There we would sit on the long wooden benches in the low dark timber stand, and stamp our feet like thunder to keep warm. Before the game started, the groundsman Mr Albert Jaggard (who was also the legendary head porter at Corpus Christi and model for Tom Sharpe's Scullion in *Porterhouse Blue*) would strut up and down in his bowler hat and gabardine raincoat, barking instructions at anyone who caught his eye. Meanwhile my father told me about the visiting teams, the mighty Cardiff or the wily Northampton and their star players, or recalled great players of the past like Wilf Wooller and Prince Obelenski. Through his work with the Fen Drainage Boards, my father knew Dickie Jeeps, the England scrum-half, whose father was a Fenland farmer.

The 'Varsity' as we called them, also had its great players who we cheered to the rafters – Gordon Waddell and Ken Scotland, Mike Gibson, and Gerald Davies. The lightweight undergraduates were often outplayed in the scrum but their twinkling backs could often run rings around their older opponents. When I too became a student, there was Jacko Page from my school, and other budding internationals like Jerry Spencer to follow.

I was not allowed to play rugby at school because of the risk of injury to my one good kidney. Football was not an official sport at the High School in the 1960s so in the Michaelmas and Lent terms I had to do cross-country running. Usually this involved a circuit starting either from the school or from the Luard Road changing rooms, out across the fields where Addenbrooke's Hospital is today to Granhams Road and Nine Wells and then back along Hills Road. We went in all weathers, and if the rugby pitches were waterlogged or snowbound, everybody had to go, stumbling across the heavy ploughed clay or the frozen clods. Some of the fat boys, of which there were few, tried to abscond by skiving off down Blinco Grove, but a master was usually placed half-way round to tick off the names. For me it was neither purgatory nor pleasure, but it wasn't enjoyable and I sympathised with Alan Sillitoe's *The Loneliness of the Long Distance Runner*.

Young cricketer, 1962. (Author's Collection)

Team games were more fun, which for me meant cricket. I was cricket-mad. As a young child I climbed into my parents' bed early in the morning to hear the crackling radio commentary of the last hour's play from the Test matches in Australia. In the garden I invented my own solitary games, throwing a tennis ball against the back wall of the outside lavatory and hitting the rebound after it had bounced on the uneven path. A cardboard box sufficed for a wicket and a straight hit into a flower bed was 'out, caught'. Thus test matches were re-enacted; Garfield Sobers, Clive Lloyd, Hall and Griffiths, Freddie Truman, Colin Cowdrey and Peter May all bestrode the back lawn, while the thumping of the ball against the brick wall drove my mother demented. I avidly read my father's books about Don Bradman and the three 'Ws' of Weekes, Worrell and Walcott, and the back numbers of the *Playfair Annual* which were on the bookshelves in the lounge.

At the County school we were organised into 'houses' for sport, Granta, Cam, Cherwell and Isis, and inter-house cricket was keenly contested. The school itself had 1st, 2nd, Colts and Minor Colts teams, through which I progressed, and there was a full fixture list through the summer, with matches against the Leys, the Perse and the Old Boys, Hitchin Grammar, Wymondham, Northampton, Woodbridge, and even Newcastle Royal Grammar. Away trips on the coach meant I had to miss Saturday morning orchestra. The competition between playing cricket and music came to a head when I broke a finger; music proved the winner.

There was always Fenner's to go and watch cricket, conveniently located on the way home from school, and admission was free for children. The head groundsman was a grumpy old chap with a limp, but the gatemen were friendly enough and let little boys like me hang around the back of the pavilion or at the nets to collect autographs. Ted Dexter, Alun Lewis and Mike Brearley all scrawled their names in my scruffy little book.

I carried on popping into Fenner's when I too was an undergraduate. Having had several lean years before then when the university team had been thrashed by every visiting county side, the presence of Majid Khan and Dudley Owen Thomas suddenly raised the standard. If word got round that Majid was batting, the lecture halls and libraries in Cambridge would empty and people would flood into Fenner's in the hope of being rewarded by a glorious century. The university even beat the visiting Pakistan tourists.

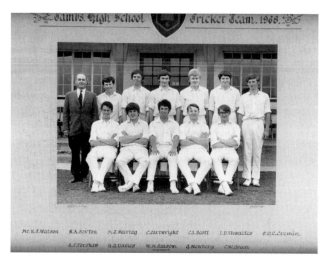

Cambs. High School Cricket Team. 1968.

Mr. K.J.Watson   R.A.Sexton   M.J.Murray   C.Cartwright   C.I.Scott   J.D.Thwaites   E.D.C.Cremin.
A.F.Forshaw   H.J.Davies   W.M.Ransom (captain)   G.Newbery   C.W.Green.

1st school cricket team, 1968.
(Author's Collection)

Sadly the delightfully shabby Edwardian pavilion was replaced in 1972 by characterless new buildings, together with undistinguished residential flats. The semi-rural old-world charm of Fenner's was lost. It is pleasing that Grange Road has not suffered a similar fate, yet.

Learning to swim was high on my parents' agenda, quite understandably given their traumatic experience in the war. I therefore joined the after-school swimming clubs at both the Perse Prep and the County, both of which used the Leys School pool. This had been built as a detached brick box, fronting Fen Causeway near the river bridge, so it had independent access. Here I was gullibly tricked by my father into swimming with less and less air in my water-wings, and eventually I did my proficiency and bronze life-saving tests. For sports day in the summer we used the unheated open-air pool at Jesus Green where the changing cubicles were 1920s Spartan and graffitied with obscenities, and there were scary tales about catching verrucas from the wet concrete floors.

Even though an indoor public pool had been promised in 1950, the new Parkside pool on Gonville Place finally opened in 1963, at a cost of £225,000. A huge bank of spectator seats was included and we all went along to the opening gala. Short-sightedly it was slightly under the new Olympic standard length, but the pool was a big attraction all year round.

I never found it an enjoyable place. The chlorine in the water was stinging on the eyes and the acoustics were deafening. The huge clear glass wall onto the road was also a somewhat voyeuristic feature, like being in an enormous goldfish bowl. Together with the horrible multi-storey car park next door it survived thirty-five years until it was replaced by a new pool, more exciting visually with its wavy roof, but geared to leisure rather than competition.

While I was growing up, football was only a fringe interest to me. Both Cambridge United, in their Abbey Road ground off Newmarket Road, and Cambridge City, behind my old Milton Road School, were non-league clubs, and I never went to see either. In the school playground there was heated rivalry between different groups of boys, but although I eagerly joined in the informal break-time games I was an outsider to their arguments. Nor did I develop any loyalty towards the big professional clubs like Manchester United or Tottenham Hotspur, as many of my class-mates did. When the results were read out on Sports Report their names remained mysterious and unimaginable. I'm sure it would have been different if I'd been brought up almost anywhere else. It is curious that Cambridge has persisted in being an unsuccessful footballing city, given its size and prosperity. The occasional cup run from Histon and their promotion to the national Conference league is more newsworthy than the exploits of the Cambridge clubs.

At school I don't believe I'd ever heard of squash rackets. Rather like Eton Fives or real tennis, squash in the 1960s was an exclusive public school pastime. My awareness of its existence coincided with my move from 'town to gown'. As a student I took it up for practical reasons it was easy to arrange a game with just one other player, there were lots of convenient and readily available courts, it was low risk for finger injury, a game didn't take long, and you could play in all weathers. It was a good choice.

As something of a weakling there was never much of a temptation for me to take up the sport which Cambridge was best at, rowing. Nor was I small enough to make a cox. Being from Bedford, my mother and grandmother liked to watch rowing and as a child I was regularly taken to see the Lent and Easter 'Bumps' at Fen Ditton. On race afternoons the banks would be crowded with casual observers like us and ardent supporters armed with hampers, boaters, plenty of liquor, banners with cryptic messages and stentorian voices. Along the gravel towpath the coaches in their blazer, caps and college colours cycled frantically beside their boats, bellowing instructions, exhortations or admonitions through their megaphones to their crews. We once saw one hapless man veer off the towpath into the river, so carried away was he with his boat. It turned out to be Canon Noel Duckworth, chaplain of Churchill.

The Bumps indeed are an unusual sport, probably unique to Cambridge and Oxford where the rivers are long but too narrow to allow boats to race side-by-side. It allows a lot of crews to participate and requires tactics and strategy, as well as speed and stamina. For me it always seemed more fun to watch than to take part.

There had been a rowing club at school which I'd known little about and when I arrived at my college, Jesus, it seemed to be a very elitist activity, highly geared towards those who'd been to public school and were already well versed in its arts. People took it incredibly seriously, got up ridiculously early in the morning to train, and formed tightly-knit cliques. Maybe that's what you had to do to succeed, and indeed three of my contemporaries at Jesus rowed in the Cambridge Boat Race Eight. Chris Ballieu went on to get a silver Olympic medal. Rowing Club dinners or Head of the River celebrations were a time to keep your head down or go elsewhere.

## CINEMA AND THEATRE

Films were not shown on television in the 1950s or '60s. Even if they had been, we didn't have a television. Instead you had to go to the cinema. My parents were not regular cinema-goers, so as a child this was a rare and incredible treat. Our nearest cinema was the Rex in Magrath Avenue, just off Victoria Road. This had the reputation for being a flea-pit, and indeed it was a dingy and grubby place. But I had no such thoughts when I went there to see my first film, *Bambi*, in 1958. We did once too have a projectionist visit the school and show black-and-white Laurel and Hardy and Buster Keaton slap-stick. *Bambi*, though, was in colour and for a seven-year-old, an enthralling and emotional experience. Sitting near the front, the screen seemed enormous, and the forest fire was terrifying.

The poshest cinema in Cambridge at that time was the Victoria on Market Hill, followed by the Regal on St Andrew's Street, where the Beatles performed in 1963. There we saw Ealing comedies such as *Genevieve* and *The Titfield Thunderbolt*, and Hollywood's *Pinnochio*, *Fantasia* and *101 Dalmatians*, but the Pearl and Dean advertisements lingered in the memory just as much as the films. I could never understand why anyone would go to the trouble of making a movie advert for the Still and Sugar Loaf wine shop, the local milkshake bar or a gentlemen's outfitters.

During those post-war decades, as television entertainment became more popular, cinemas were closing, the Art Deco Central in Hobson Street (now a bingo hall), the Tivoli in Chesterton

Road (now the Graduate pub) and the Playhouse in Mill Road (now the Salvation Army shop). With smaller audiences, the big single-screen cinemas were unprofitable, magnificent though they were for new productions like *Lawrence of Arabia* when it came out in 1962. As a student I turned my attention to the Arts Cinema, tiny and uncomfortable, tucked away in Market Passage. This showed non-Hollywood films, run very much on the independent lines of the Academy or Everyman Cinemas in London, with a high turnover of art-house films and late night specials. This was the place to see Bunuel, Bergman, Truffaut, and Hitchcock, even if you did come out with a stiff neck and cramp in your legs. It was here that I first saw such epics as *The Seven Samurai* and *Les Enfants du Paradis*.

Sadly, none of the old cinemas in central Cambridge have survived. The Victoria beside the market lies empty while the Regal was converted into a Wetherspoon's pub. The Arts Cinema was redeveloped in 1999 for new shops and coffee bars, and there is no trace of the old Rex. The Kinema in Mill Road, near the junction with Gwydir Street was finally demolished in 1996, having been derelict for years. Instead the fashion now is for out-of-town multi-screen multiplex cinemas. Cineworld, built on the site of the old cattle market off Cherry Hinton Road and the Vue/Warner Village complex on East Road fit this mould. Fortunately there is the new four-screen Arts Picturehouse in St Andrew's Street, above the old Regal, which caters for Cambridge film buffs, and hosts the annual Cambridge film festival.

My parents were far more interested in the theatre, and saw most of the productions which visited the Arts Theatre, as well as following the career of my actor-uncle John. I was first taken to see Gilbert and Sullivan whose most popular operettas were put on every year for several weeks before Christmas by the Cambridge Amateur Operatic Society. They were directed by the genial bespectacled Eric Wedd, who looked like our bank manager, and the cast was made up of townsfolk. The star of the show, every year, was the leading man, Roy Braybrooke, who was dashing, sang in tune and rattled off the patter-songs.

I loved the Arts Theatre, shoe-horned as it was behind the facades of Peas Hill and St Edwards Passage. It was a hidden world of plush carpets and red velvet drapes, chandeliers, gilt decoration, seats which tipped back when you stood up, and a steep rake to the auditorium which focussed all attention on the tiny stage. It was grand, yet intimate.

My own theatrical initiation came at the more austere ADC theatre in Park Street, behind the Round Church. In 1963 I was dragooned by Denis Fielder into a production of Menotti's *Amahl and the Night Visitors*. After a whole term of rehearsals there were eight shows in one week before Christmas. Together with Andrew Fielder and Randal Keynes I was one of the shepherds, but also had to understudy the part of Amahl. Denis and Molly Gilmour provided the 'orchestra' on two pianos. Mari Bicknell, who ran the Cambridge Ballet workshop, was in charge of the dancers, and the overall producer was Gabor Cossa, a generously proportioned man who ran an antique shop in Trumpington Street. With his heavily indulged Italian accent and his histrionic mannerisms he seemed to be the epitome of a theatrical director, and a dead-ringer for Zero Mostel in *The Producers*.

The ADC was utilitarian, with none of the plushness or comforts of the Arts. Everything was black, the walls and floors, the curtains and drapes, and there was the distinctive theatrical smell which comes from dust, hot spot lights, scenery paint, glue and make-up. Backstage was incredibly cramped and chaotic with wardrobe ladies clucking over costumes, ballerinas doing their exercises and nervous young singers like me trying to remember their lines. After such excitement the school plays seemed rather tame.

Music provided the way for me into theatre. In 1967 I was an on-stage musician in the Mummers May Week production of Ben Jonson's *The Alchemist*, put on in the cloisters of Jesus College. At the time I had no idea that I might end up here as a student. Among the cast, playing Pertinax Surly, was a student called Salman Rushdie. This was my first encounter with Graham Ripley, who had written the music.

Graham taught at the Cambridge College of Arts and Technology, or the 'Tech.' as we knew it, and the following year I encountered him again in the Graduate Theatre Society (GROTS) production of *Oh What a Lovely War*, again at the ADC. John Richens had asked me, Michael Cole and Jo Burton to help with arrangements of the music. Graham lived life at 100 miles an hour, and that included his driving. After two weeks in Cambridge we took the show out to Linton Village College, and on one journey home, with several of us in the back seat, we went straight over, literally, the roundabout outside Abington. Graham had his fingers in many pies, real and speculative artistic ventures, and always hoped that he would make his fortune by writing a West End musical. In 1970 he organised the music for the Footlights' show, *Gone with the Clappers*, with Clive James, but soon afterwards he left Cambridge. Some said he went to be a pig farmer in Northamptonshire, but that might have been a flying-pig story.

Once I'd become competent on the bassoon I was invited to play in the opera orchestra for the G&S in the Arts, and saw it all from the other side – the discreet stage door in St Edwards Passage, the narrow corridors and miniscule band room, the bone-dry acoustic and lack of elbow room in the pit, the hazards of the music stand lights and the trailing wires, the murmuring hubbub of the audience before the show, the hushed expectancy as the lights went down, the frustration of not being able to see the action on stage. Much of course has been improved since then, with the roof-top bar and café and the 1996 overhaul which enhanced the front-of-house and backstage, but happily it left the 1936 auditorium (paid for, incidentally, by John Maynard Keynes) intact.

The ADC has changed out of recognition. Now actually part of the university, a phased development from 2000 to 2008 has seen a new street façade, new dressing rooms, green rooms and a set workshop behind the scenes, and smart comfortable raked seats in the auditorium. Luxury indeed!

# REMEMBRANCE

As a young child, with no grasp of history and no real understanding of the passage of time, I did not realise how recent the Second World War had been. Our house and its immediate surrounds showed few scars of war. Cambridge town too was not pock-marked with bomb sites, and indeed had escaped comparatively lightly from enemy action. Vicarage Terrace, off East Road, had been worst hit, in an early raid in 1940. More damage had been done by 'friendly fire' from British or American planes ditching their bombs or incendiaries before an emergency landing. There were a few clusters of pre-fabs to house those made homeless, including some nearby in Histon Road

In the surrounding countryside the legacy of the war effort was everywhere to be seen. The aerodromes at Oakington, Waterbeach, Bourn, Graveley, Wyton, Bassingbourne, Fowlmere and Duxford were just a few of the hundreds of air bases hastily constructed or enlarged in East Anglia just before or during the war, covering thousands of acres of former farmland with miles of concrete runways and standing bays. Cambridgeshire with its flat landscape had more than its fair share.

Some of these airfields were already disused, with grass growing through the joints in the concrete, and the hangers standing like great black sentinels against the skyline. At Bourn we learnt to drive, and the more adventurous went land-yachting. The footpath to Coton from Wilberforce Road skirted in right-angles around the old ammunition depot with its sinister corrugated shed, fenced off with barbed wire at concrete posts. An accidental explosion here in 1960 greatly alarmed all those within ear-shot. The new cycle path still takes this circuitous route even though the hanger and its dangerous contents have long gone.

During the 1950s many of the air bases were still in use. At Bassingbourn there were Canberra bombers and at Waterbeach there were Javelins and Hawker Hunters and, later, Lightning jet fighters. Although the planes have gone some of the concrete walls erected as Cold War blast shelters still survive. Whenever we drove up the A1 north of Peterborough, we stared with trepidation at the serried ranks of Bloodhound missiles, all pointing east.

On a Saturday every September, we went to an air display to celebrate Battle of Britain Day, usually at Duxford, Bassingbourn or Waterbeach. There we watched fly-passes of Spitfires and Hurricanes, Lancasters and Wellingtons, and had our ear drums shattered by the roar of the latest Vulcan, Victor or Valliant bomber screaming low overhead. There were often parachutes drops, aiming to land within a target, and demonstration of RAF police dogs, jumping through hoops or catching a well-padded 'intruder'.

All this was great fun for a little boy. So too was 'Poppy Day' or 'Rag Day' in early November when the whole of central Cambridge became a carnival, and all the town and gown would turn out to participate or spectate. This event had started in 1922 as a way of raising money for the Earl Haig Fund and the injured veterans of the First World War, and by the 1950s was one of Cambridge's great traditions. The main feature was a huge procession of floats, flat trailers drawn by lorries, tractors and traction engines, one for every college and town institution, which were decorated or dressed up as sets on which students acted out bizarre or fantastical cameos. My father would lift me onto his shoulders so that I could see over the press of the crowd. There were brass bands, jazz bands, Dixie bands, and marching bands, merging like a Charles Ives' score, while people in fancy dress mingled in the throng, collecting money in buckets. There were stalls and stunts, such as piano-smashing competitions, jugglers on stilts and tight-rope walkers.

In the 1950s there were still plenty of disabled victims from the First World War, men still in their sixties or seventies. Cambridge had its share of tramps and vagrants, none more memorable than Jock, who wore a fisherman's jumper and a woolly hat and jogged around Cambridge, occasionally shouting nonsense at passers-by. He slept in a garage owned by some kind-hearted people in Trumpington, and it was said that he'd never recovered from shell-shock. Then there was Trevor, who hung around the fountain in the Market Place, usually with a bottle in his hand. Apparently he appeared a record 113 times before the city bench before his demise in 1978.

'Moral rearmament', in front of Joshua Taylor, 1961. (Author's Collection)

The American Cemetery, Madingley.

By the late 1960s students began to tire of such philanthropy, probably linked to the growing anti-war and anti-Vietnam movement, and the police and local magistrates became less tolerant of pranks and skirmishes between students and local youth. Rag Day fizzled out and was barely in evidence when my turn came to be a student.

As a child, I was taught to wear my poppy with pride and to believe that Winston Churchill was the greatest living Englishman, particularly after I'd seen the stooping giant in the flesh. We often visited the American Cemetery at Madingley and marvelled at the neat ranks of white crosses and Jewish stars fanning out across the immaculate lawns. I would stare at the huge world map murals in the chapel which depicted the Allies campaigns; we would throw coins into the shallow pool outside and walk past the endless names carved into the long Portland stone wall.

In the summer of 1965 the sounds of the war suddenly came close to home with the aerial re-enactments for the film of *The Battle of Britain*. Duxford was used as the base (before its runway was shortened by the construction of the M11 motorway), and huge numbers of antique Heinkels and Dorniers were hired or borrowed from Franco's ageing Spanish air force to replicate the great German bomber raids of the Blitz. Lessons at school were regularly abandoned as pupils and teachers alike rushed out to gape at the massed formations droning overhead, and the vapour trails from the reconstructed dogfights between Spitfires and Messerschmitts.

My grandmother was openly anti-German. That same summer she embarrassed everyone by making un-PC comments in front of poor Christoph, our exchange student from Heidelberg. After my mother's remonstrations she went back to Bedford in a huff. My parents were patriotic but bore no grudges, even though they both had good reason to remember the war. My mother's brother Michael had been killed in 1945, and was buried in Kiel War Cemetery. My brother, born the following year, was christened Michael, but called by his second name Roger because my grandmother couldn't bear it. My father's favourite cousin Alec Macdonald had been killed in Burma in 1943, one of Wingate's jungle warriors. Less than eight years later I was named accordingly in his honour.

# REBELLION

Rebellion is a normal part of the process of growing up, challenging the established constraints of home, school, family and society. On the face of it there was little for me to rebel against; we were warm and well fed, lived in a nice house with a garden, and had lots of things to look forward to like Christmas, birthdays and summer holidays. My parents were happy and devoted to their children. It is strange how the contentment and acceptance of early childhood, cocooned in the comforts and reassurance of domestic life, can turn into the dissatisfaction and churlish frustration of adolescence, much of it unfounded and later to be regretted.

Like most children I disliked the constant exhortation for hygiene from my mother. 'Don't touch that, it's filthy dirty', 'make sure you wash your hands', 'brush your hair', 'have you got a clean handkerchief?' were phrases which became resented through over-familiarity. My grandmother said that cleanliness was next to godliness, but frankly I had little enthusiasm for either. She also tried to frighten us with stories of how when she was a 'naughty little girl', her mother once locked her in a cupboard and forgot about her. It seemed an unlikely threat.

Being made to wear my brother's cast-off clothes was another source of grievance. I never seemed to stand a chance of catching up. Everything was darned or patched, kept going as long as possible. Shirts, jumpers and trousers which were no longer smart enough for church or school were relegated to gardening duties, or ultimately became rags or cleaning cloths. Nothing was thrown away. On reflection it was perfectly understandable at the time. Compared to today's cheap imports, new clothes and shoes in the 1950s and '60s were expensive, and unaffordable on a tight budget. They were made to last a life-time, and my parents ensured they did.

I also kicked against the family rules and rituals of Sunday church, Sunday afternoon walks, bedtime, not being allowed to play on the grass when it was wet, and having to help with the washing up. Meeting other children at school and in the Holiday Orchestra, glimpsing the artistic world of Denis Fielder, seeing the bright lights of London with my bohemian uncle, joining the National Youth Orchestra, all these adventures opened my eyes and provoked seeds of envy or disgruntlement with one's own lot.

At school I was a compliant pupil, and being small but nimble I kept out of the way of gangs, bullies and miscreants. Mercifully, I never got seriously mixed up with the smokers behind the bike sheds. My father had smoked cigarettes and then a pipe and liked the occasional cigar, but my mother never did. Plenty of visitors to our house smoked, especially my grandmother, and we had ash trays liberally dotted around. Naturally in due course I tried cigarettes, especially in the NYO where it was a popular subversive activity, but I never liked it, and never got hooked on the nicotine. I couldn't have afforded to; 2s pocket money per week, even when I was eighteen, didn't go very far.

At school, drugs and knives were unknown and not the bane of the playground as they can be today. Glue sniffing which some of the kids did in the bushes behind Drummer Street bus station seemed to be the worst possible thing you could do. It seemed unappealing, particularly if you got your nose stuck to the lid. Even at university I was ignorant or oblivious of any drugs in Jesus College; perhaps I was simply naive or not part of that 'set'. Only in my second year when I fraternised with NYO friends at King's and Corpus did I become aware of marijuana, cocaine and LSD, and the idea of getting stoned.

Alcohol was always a more attractive option. Geography field-trips, CCF camp and National Youth Orchestra courses all offered the chance for 'escape' to a pub, the frisson of under-age drinking and the opportunity to sample beer or stranger concoctions.

In the sixth-form John Richens and I had more free time than most, as we did my A-Level Music outside school hours. Apart from getting good at table tennis in the prefects' common room, we took to hanging around at the Tech., more properly known as the Cambridgeshire College of Arts and Technology. At that time this was the nearest thing in Cambridge to a sixth-form college. It conveyed a liberal and grown-up feeling, free of uniforms or petty regulations, and most importantly, had girls. The shabby portacabins in Bradmore Street became a new mecca. Michael Cole had already left school to study there, but I made new friends such as Chris Bullen who'd come from the Perse and Jonathan (Jo) Burton who'd moved with his parents to Maids Causeway from Hitchin.

The music department attracted some unusually influential characters, such as the quixotic Graham Ripley and the inspirational John Myatt, who taught woodwind. Norman Hearn was nominally in charge, and conducted the Tech. orchestra in which I was soon playing the bassoon alongside Jo, but his two daughters, Juliette and Phyllida, were his most appreciated asset. One of the concerts was in Impington Village College, only a mile or so from home and whose buildings seemed unremarkable to an untutored eye. It was extraordinary to be told that they had been designed in 1936 by an architect, Walter Gropius, who had been married to Gustav Mahler's wife and the death of whose daughter in 1934 had inspired Alban Berg's *Violin Concerto*.

At home there were predictable verbal tussles with parents wanting to know where I'd been and what time I would be back. Our little house now seemed like a strait-jacket; Histon Road seemed shabby and undesirable. I envied friends who lived in bigger houses or smarter streets. I used the excuse of piano practice as a reason for not going to church on Sunday mornings, when at least I could have the house to myself. Occasionally, to let off steam I went on long bike rides, out through Girton to Madingley, Coton, Granchester and Trumpington, or through Impington to Milton, Clayhithe, Horningsea and Fen Ditton. At least it was a good way of getting to know the necklace of villages around Cambridge and the network of what then were quiet country lanes, as yet unsullied by badly driven 4x4s and land cruisers, zipping to and from out-of-town superstores.

Like most teenagers I was wrapped up in my own little world, unconscious of much that was going on elsewhere. The 1960s were a decade whose tone was determined by a rising generation; youthful optimism was shaping music, fashion, technology and politics. Like my friends I wanted to grow my hair long, and have flared trousers and winkle-picker shoes, but at home, at school and around town I was largely sheltered from much more than this. I heard about mods and rockers, skinheads and greasers, but didn't actually know any. David Lane and Sir Francis Pym held the City and County as safe Tory seats with seemingly little prospect for change.

In the town there were outbreaks of vandalism, and fights between students and local yobs – grad bashing as it was known. Town kids would stand on bridges and throw water bombs at punts, or steal poles from the unwary. There were student high jinks, such as in June 1958 when an Austin Seven van was erected overnight on the roof of the Senate House (it took several days for the authorities to get it down), and the *Cambridge Daily News* remarked that it was a solution to the town's parking problems. In June 1965, Vietnam protest banners were strung between the pinnacles of King's College Chapel. In November 1967 300 students demonstrated when the American ambassador visited Churchill College. In January 1969 students occupied the Old Schools in solidarity with a sit-in at the London School of Economics. Reforms and relaxation to gate hours and an end to the university's over-representation on the City Council were demanded. Compared to the near-revolutions of 1968 in Paris or the assassination of Martin Luther King, it seems trivial now.

As a student I suddenly became much better informed, even if the 1960s had passed me by. Everybody had posters of Che Guevara or Fidel Castro on their walls, and Tariq Ali was a cult figure. In February 1970 the riot at the Garden House Hotel, following the picketing of a 'Greek evening' supported by the colonels' right-wing regime, caused a great stir. The dinner was invaded and the interior badly damaged as police and demonstrators fought. The bulldogs and proctors, who were the university's own police force, were called in to give evidence at the trial of the nine arrested ring-leaders, six of whom were sent to prison. The Garden

June, 1958.
(Cambridge Newspapers Ltd)

Rag Day stunt.
(Cambridge Newspapers Ltd)

House Hotel never really recovered. In 1972 it was burnt down, accidentally, and has now been hideously rebuilt as the new Doubletree Hilton.

In February 1972 there were further sit-ins in the Old Schools, led by activists from King's, and violent clashes between students and constables. Demands were made for representation for students on the Faculty Boards, changes in methods of assessment, recognition of the Cambridge Students' Union, and abolition of the dreaded proctors. For those not involved there was much discussion in college bars, left and right wingers cutting their political teeth, and a certain amount of puzzled apathy and outrage in the local press.

It did not take me long to pass from 'town' to 'gown'. Ironically, almost symbolically, in my first term as a student I was set upon by a group of thugs as I cycled late one night down Garret Hostel Lane. I recognised two of the lads from school, but they weren't interested in my pleading that I was a really a townie, like them. I managed to run away, but my bike ended up in the river.

## WEST CAMBRIDGE

As my awareness of the town and university developed I became increasingly attracted to west Cambridge. I had learnt in Geography lessons at schools that in Britain, because of the prevailing westerly winds, most cities had their industry on the east side so that the smoke would not blow across the town. That indeed was the case in Cambridge, not that there was actually any heavy industry giving off obnoxious smells, but the railway with its steam engines, the gas works, the sewage farm at Chesterton and what industry there was were all on the east side, together with Marshalls airport, the cemetery and the football grounds.

West Cambridge, by which I mean the swathe from Huntingdon Road to Trumpington Road west of the Backs, was, by contrast, occupied by university institutions, such as the library and the Sidgwick site, Newnham and Selwyn colleges, and lots of large houses with big gardens. It was an area full of green spaces and sports grounds, which merged into open fields and meadows beyond. My favourite bicycle route home from school was to cut across Lammas Land, Sheeps Green and Coe Fen to Newnham and then along Grange Road and Storeys Way to Huntingdon Road.

Nikolaus Pevsner in his 1954 survey described this area as the 'Villenviertel' of Cambridge, comparing it nostalgically to the pre-war villa districts of Berlin. Only later did I come to realise that this eclectic collection of buildings included some of the finest late Victorian and inter-war 'moderne' architecture in England. At the time I knew nothing about styles such as Arts and Crafts or Art Deco, nor of architects such as Baillie Scott or Marshall Sissons, George Checkley or his pupil Dora Cosens. I was however entranced by the grandeur of many of the mansions and villas, and fascinated by the rich mixture and variety of materials and features. Some of the houses had handsome or whimsical names, such as Squerryes and Lennel in Storeys Way, Five Gables and Upton House in Grange Road. To me these huge houses with their sweeping clay tile roofs, pretty dormers, hipped gables and prominent upright chimneys seemed idyllic. Some had elaborately carved door cases, one with a heavy round hood; some had leaded light windows, others had windows of all shapes and sizes, almost randomly arranged. Most were set well back from the road, with spacious gardens and high hedges, a gravel drive for the Lagonda, and a backcloth of huge trees. Most of all I liked No.48 Storeys Way, with its topiary in the front garden.

My father's boss, Walter Doran, lived in one of the smaller and plainer houses in Wilberforce Road, but on the opposite side were some very different homes, sparklingly white, crisply square-edged, flat-roofed, and distinctly modern. They had large windows with narrow metal frames, and one, No.9, had a flat canopy to shade its roof-top patio. My parents thought they

No. 48 Storeys Way, by Baillie Scott.(Cambridge 2000)

would be very uncomfortable to live in, 'with all that glass'. 'Think of the cost of the curtains' my mother remarked. I was inclined to think otherwise. The Richens family lived in Barton Close, one of a group of utilitarian brick houses built after the war when materials were scarce. Their large Crittall windows seemed to let in lots of light. Christine Boyes, who was one of the girls at the Tech. lived in the even more sequestered Selwyn Gardens. The hospitable Buffery family, several of whom played in the Holiday Orchestra, lived in Clarkson Road, close neighbours of Fred Hoyle.

West Cambridge also included the old hamlet of Newnham Croft and the start of the footpath out across the meadows to Grantchester. The village was less beset with tourists than it is today. The four pubs had not yet been tarted up or expanded to do posh food, and the Rose and Crown had not changed its name to the Rupert Brooke. At the junction of the High Street and Coton Road the row of picturesque cottage had not yet been saved from demolition and restored. The Orchard tea rooms were popular during May Week, but low-key and uncommercialised. There was even talk of closure and redeveloped for housing. The Old Vicarage next door was also unmodernised, and behind the peeling shutters one could imagine that Rupert Brooke might still lodge there and that 'Oh! Yet stands the church clock at ten to three'. Not until 1980 was it bought and done up by Jeffery and Mary Archer. Beyond the mill race, further upstream, few people bothered to find Byron's Pool where in the shade of gnarled willows kingfishers could be seen darting along the river banks. Before the construction of the noisy Western bypass, Michael Hopkins' tent-like Schlumberger building and Ted Cullinan's Maths campus, the footpath out to Coton from the end of Adams Road was equally deserted, often overgrown with brambles and weeds heaving through the cracked concrete slabs.

These may seem nostalgic and youthful impressions, but there are not without some foundation. Much has happened in west Cambridge – the massive expansion of the University Library with its huge new stacks, the enlargement of Churchill, Newnham and Fitzwilliam colleges, the extensions to King's choir school, the transformation of the Sidgwick site, the building of Wolfson and Darwin colleges and Clare Hall. For a short while as a student I taught the bassoon to a boy, one of the New family who lived in a huge house on Grange Road next to the junction with Hershel Road, opposite where the Bin Brook briefly emerges from its culvert on its way to join the Cam. The father worked for the British Council and travelled up to London, which was unusual then. This house together with several others which were pulled down was to become part of the new Robinson College, built in 1979, and Cambridge's most recent new undergraduate college.

Despite all this the area remains the most pleasant part of Cambridge. The wonderful villas by H.C. Hughes in Millington Road, still with its gas-lit street lamps, survive as a testament to the academic emancipation and wealth of the early twentieth-century university. The muddy Cam and its backwaters still glide along behind the rear gardens of Grantchester Meadows, children on hot summer days swim and splash in the river, jumping off the Sheep's Green footbridge.. and there is still honey for tea.

## *NEW ARCHITECTURE*

Cambridge experienced a huge surge of new building in the 1960s, mainly among the colleges and university. I was aware of this not just because of the cranes and cement mixers, all of which were very interesting to a boy, but because my parents, and most of their conservative-minded friends and acquaintances, talked about little else. After all the anxieties and disturbance of the leviathan Arbury Estate, the apparent desecration of the Cambridge colleges was the last straw.

The amount of new development was phenomenal. After two decades of economic inactivity, because of the war and its legacy of shortages and austerity, there was pent-up energy for change both in the university and the town. Among the colleges a new breed of dons and commissioning committees were keen to stamp their mark and break new ground. In 1954 Pevsner had described recent collegiate buildings (including the 1930s) as 'sadly insignificant' or 'timidly imitative'. In January 1958 the *Architects' Journal* had proclaimed, emphatically, that 'there are no notable post-war buildings in Cambridge'. That was all to change.

Probably the biggest and most anticipated addition was Churchill College, the first new men's college to be built in Cambridge for seventy years. It had been a brain-child of Sir Winston back in 1955 shortly after he resigned as prime minister, and in 1958 forty acres of farmland between Madingley Road and Storeys Way were acquired. For the architects, Sheppard Robson, this was the opportunity of a lifetime, commissioned as they were with the brief 'to build a college for scientists with the medieval certainty to last a thousand years'. The building site

The Erasmus Building, Queens' College, 1967. (Author's Collection)

became a familiar landmark, something we passed very regularly. As the first blocks and the main entrance on Storeys Way took shape in 1960, so did the criticisms. My father likened the residential blocks with their projecting balconies to a piece of furniture with half the drawers pulled out at random. The huge blank brick walls of the entrance portico and the chapel brought scathing comments from my mother: 'it looks like the squash courts'. Neither of them liked the rough-hewn brick or chunky exposed slabs of roughly shuttered concrete. At the time it was intended that Madingley Road would be made into a dual carriageway, hence the wide strip of grass and, later, trees.

The new Fitzwilliam College on Huntingdon Road which started in 1961 evoked similarly stinging comments. 'When is it going to have a roof?' or 'it looks like a prison' were typical remarks. In hindsight, it was one of Denys Lasdun's calmer efforts, particularly compared to what was to come in 1968 with his wilfully raked new range at Christ's. While some architectural critics praised the way this radical terraced design addressed the inside of the college, no-one had a good word to say about how it looked from King Street – a series of ugly concrete overhangs, uninviting voids and access ramps to the underground car park. It was the antithesis of a good street frontage and incurred outrage from townspeople.

For my parents, the most controversial new building was the Erasmus Building at Queens', the first along the Backs in the modernist style. As college bursar, our near neighbour and fellow church-goer Walter Hagenbuch happened to be on the Building Committee who had commissioned Sir Basil Spence in 1958, and he gave us a blow-by-blow account. Of course, many people including my mother, thought that the views across the meadows and gardens from Queens' Road were sacrosanct, but the pressure for expansion won the day. The five proposed storeys were eventually reduced to three, but the fact that these sat on stilts and were capped with a prominent roof top pergola only fuelled the furore. The greenery which made the pergola look attractive on the plans never materialised for lack of an automated watering system. Nearer to our church, at the bottom of Little St Mary's Lane, the new Graduate Centre attracted similar criticism for its excessive scale next to the old pub and the Mill Pond.

In 1966 Ralph Lapwood, fellow of St John's, gave us an early tour around the nearly finished Cripps Building which fronted daringly onto the river near Magdalene Bridge. He was quizzical about how the honey-combed Portland limestone would weather (although after forty years the architects Powell and Moya have been thoroughly vindicated).

We all had a good laugh when some pranksters stencilled large black footprints on the pristine white dome of the recently completed New Hall.

In West Road we had been perplexed by the blank walls and peripheral catwalks of Harvey Court, the new residential complex for Gonville and Caius. My father said that it looked 'as though it had landed from outer-space'. Leslie Martin and Colin St John Wilson had indeed set out to create an introverted fortress, a haven of tranquillity for those living inside, although Ralph Erskine at Clare Hall showed how you could do this in a more humane, less brutal manner.

None of this prepared us or anyone else for what happened further along West Road, in the gardens where our church summer parties had been held. James Stirling's 1968 History Faculty, with its fierce red Accrington brick, obsessively chamfered, and its huge walls of glass, made everyone draw breath, and probably still does. As Pevsner wrote soon after, 'people in 2068 will shake their heads at such self-confidence'.

The town also had plenty of new buildings, much sadly very mediocre. Close to home the Arbury Estate had tried, laudably, to create a new 'village' with its own shops, pub, church and schools, but it had failed by sprawling too far and the architecture was exceedingly weak; prim brick terraces with flush utility doors, concrete garage courts with up-and-over doors, and expansive but unusable grass verges. Kings Hedges was even worse.

The new Police Station and swimming pool facing Parker's Piece had a little more pizzazz, even the new offices for the Great Ouse River Board in Clarendon Road, but there was little to match the quality of Eric Lyons' stylish Highsett on Hills Road. Probably the best new commercial building in the centre of Cambridge in the '60s was Heffers' new shop on Trinity Street, replacing the old Matthews grocery store. With its spacious central well and four levels of stacks and shelves it was completely different from any previous bookshop in Cambridge, 'a new retail experience' as it would be hyped today. More of that was to come, much less pleasantly, in the 1970s with the ghastly Kite and Lion Yard developments.

The indigestibility and sheer volume of new architecture in the 1960s perhaps took the edge of everybody's critical faculties in the following decade. In the splurge of new university buildings, the affluent budgets coupled with a degree of snobbery among the dons meant that most of the great names of British architects designed something in Cambridge. Local architects were largely overlooked. The result was often an overstated striving for effect, unbridled individuality, over-dramatic and uncontextual. Today there is nowhere better than Cambridge to see the variety of 1960s architecture, but as Pevsner put it, there are elephants as well as butterflies.

# KETTLE'S YARD

The visual arts and museums were not major interests of my parents. I vaguely remember as a young child being taken by my mother into the Fitzwilliam Museum and being rather scared by the immensity of the spaces and spooked by the William Blake paintings. Not understanding what I was looking at, and constantly being told to keep quiet in a place where the tiniest whisper was magnified by the echoing marble, made a poor impression. I liked the stone lions outside best of all.

We went more frequently to the Scott Polar Research Institute Museum in Lensfield Road, where I learnt about the heroic and doomed expeditions of Franklin and Scott, Titus Oates and Wilson. I saw Amundsen's flag from the South Pole and the actual sno-cat with which Sir Vivian Fuchs, who lived in Barton Road, had travelled across Antartica in 1958. As a small boy, human endurance seemed more interesting than artistic endeavour.

We also went to the Folk Museum at the bottom of Castle Hill where by contrast the floors were creaky, the rooms dark, dusty and pokey and the exhibits dingy and excruciatingly boring to a seven-year-old.

While I was still at school I had barely heard of Kettle's Yard. I think I imagined it was probably part of the Folk Museum. However in 1968, when I was in the sixth-form, my piano teacher Denis Fielder invited me to attend a recital to be given by the Macnaghten Quartet. Denis told me to come to his house in Chesterton Road first, so that we could go together. As we walked along Chesterton Lane he explained that Kettle's Yard was a private house, lived in by a gentleman who collected art and liked from time to time to have music in his house, to which he invited his friends. Anne Macnaghten knew Denis well and had asked for a couple of places.

My parents, to their great credit, had already taken me to lots of concerts. We'd been several times to hear the London Mozart Players in the Guildhall, conducted by Harry Blech ('bleary hack' as my London uncle called him) and had heard Thea King and Janet Craxton as soloists. I'd been mesmerised by Peter Katin's piano recital in the Arts Theatre when he'd played the Liszt *Sonata* and Debussy's *Images*, and by Leon Goossens when he performed with Andrew Davies on harpsichord in King's Chapel. I'd been enthralled by Carl Pini's London String Quartet, again at the Arts. Every year from 1963 to 1969 we went up to London to see a cricket

Kettle's Yard, from
Northampton Street.

match at Lord's (usually the Gillette Cup) and then a Promenade concert at the Albert Hall. There we'd seen Malcolm Sargent ('flash Harry' as my father called him) conduct the BBC Symphony Orchestra and Stokowski, just as flashy, direct the New Philharmonia. My uncle had taken me to the Royal Opera House, so I'd been more fortunate than most.

Kettle's Yard, however, was something else. The evening was enchanting, not only for the music which was more intimate than anything I'd experienced before, but more because of the interior of the house and the whole extraordinary atmosphere of exotic objects, beautiful furniture and rugs. The house had a tremendous sense of calm and well-being. Jim Ede greeted us at the front door, tall and slightly bent, but with a wide smile and a shake of my mitt with his big bony hand. Everyone spoke quietly and knowledgeably. During the concert people sat or perched on window seats, benches, chairs and cushions on the floor. At the end I left still in a trance. I hadn't known such a place could exist.

Afterwards I found out more about the genial H.S. 'Jim' Ede; that he'd been a boy at the Leys School, and that he'd moved back to Cambridge in 1956 after a nomadic life. He'd bought three run-down cottages off Castle Hill behind St Peter's church and in 1957 knocked them together to create a house for himself and gallery for his collection of twentieth-century art and sculpture. Here he operated an 'open house', invited friends and students, sharing and communicating his personal taste and morality, and hosting concerts.

In 1967, by now aged seventy-two, Jim bequeathed Kettle's Yard and its contents to the university, and it was decided to build an extension onto the cottages to house more adequately his wonderful collection of Ben Nicolson, Henry Moore, Joan Miro, Barbara Hepworth and Henri Gaudier-Brzeska ( the enigmatic 'Savage Messiah'). The design brief was a great challenge, to provide more space without spoiling the unique karma of the place. Leslie Martin's solution was both sympathetic and beguiling, arguably his finest contribution to Cambridge. To celebrate the completion in 1969-70, there were concerts, and a ballot was held for tickets. I was one of the few who applied for the allocation to Jesus College, and was lucky each time. Thus I came to sit cross-legged on the polished beige brick floor almost at the feet of a youthful Jacqueline Du Pres and Daniel Barenboim, and again for the recital of late Beethoven piano sonatas by Claudio Arrau. In 1972 I saw the virtuoso oboist Heinz Holliger and his harpist wife Ursula.

It was quite a surprise the following year when Jim Ede left Kettle's Yard and Cambridge, to live in Edinburgh. Although he gave more pieces to the collection he never once came back. In Scotland he started a 'new life', and spent his time as a hospital visitor, until his death in 1990, aged ninety-four.

Inevitably Kettle's Yard has a less personal feel now, although it remains one of Cambridge's loveliest gems. Today there is a larger extension, designed by Bland Brown and Cole in 1994, with a shop, temporary exhibitions and a café fronting onto the Castle Street, and a projecting sign outside to lure the visitor. Even more ambitious extensions are now proposed with an appeal for £5 million. But those who know can still go and ring the bell on the little cottage door where every afternoon (except Mondays) someone will let you in. Then you can wander through the house and still feel much of the magic which Jim left behind.

## JESUS COLLEGE

It may seem an odd, even unwise decision to go to a university in your home town. In my case I wasn't given much of a choice, and it didn't seem an unnatural thing to do. At my school there was unbridled ambition among the teachers to achieve Oxbridge places and a strong bias in favouring Cambridge as opposed to 'the other place'. Four years earlier my brother had been to Queens' to study Natural Sciences, and my parents were keen as mustard that I should follow in his footsteps. Getting a degree and 'a good job', rather than pursuing music as a career, was seen as the number one priority. Without doubt they regarded getting both their boys into Cambridge University as the best possible accolade of their parenting.

At school I had grown to like and do well in Geography, and in September 1968, with A-Levels still nine months away I was put in for the Jesus College entrance exam, and sent for an interview with Bruce Sparks, eminent geomorphologist and Director of Studies for Geography of Jesus. I was somewhat surprised and relieved that the interview involved very few questions about my chosen subject and much more about my interests and hobbies. We talked for twenty minutes about operas and orchestras. The subsequent offer of a place took all the pressure off my final two terms at school. I was lucky; unlike most of my contemporaries I

The Chimney; the entrance off Jesus Lane.

avoided the chore and worry of filling in UCAS forms, and deciding what my second and third choices would be.

Compared to the string of colleges along the 'Backs', Jesus is off the beaten track. Usually when my parents took visitors around the colleges, it was Magdalene, St John's, Trinity, Clare, Trinity Hall, King's and Queens'. Jesus was unfamiliar territory, although I had ventured in before to perform in the Mummers' play and once to visit my school friend John Sharpe's father's rooms. Dr Alan Sharpe was a chemist, fellow and Tutor for Admissions. He also happened to be mad about opera, especially Mozart, and spent most of his free time whizzing off to Glyndebourne or Salzburg. I am sure he looked kindly on my entry.

The main entrance and gatehouse is substantially set back from Jesus Lane, approached down the long external corridor known as 'the Chimney', lined with high brick walls behind which lie the privacy of the Fellows' garden and the Master's Lodge. The college is blessed with spacious grounds, inherited from the gardens and orchards of the nunnery on which the college was founded in 1496. Unlike any of the other central Cambridge colleges, Jesus has all its buildings and playing fields together, the rugby and football pitches facing Victoria Road, the cricket ground with its pretty 1930s thatched pavilion and backcloth of trees screening it from Jesus Green. Apart from the ancient cloisters, all its courtyards are open on at least one side, a tradition that has been maintained even with recent developments.

In the autumn of 1969 the squash courts were newly opened, and North Court, designed by local architect David Roberts, was only five years old. Unlike many of the older buildings, North Court had all mod-cons, with clusters of four bedrooms sharing a kitchen, showers and washrooms.

All 127 first year undergraduates were accommodated in college, and I was provided with a ground floor room, 2CC2, in the far corner of Chapel Court. Baths and hot water were in the basement on the other side, a hundred yards away, but I didn't mind. At least no-one had to share; everyone had their own room, and after my tiny bedroom at home, mine felt like a palace.

The first few weeks were a shock to the system. Despite having longed to get away from home, and despite being in my home town, I felt like a fish out of water. Probably many others did too, some more so, but those who'd been to boarding schools seemed more at ease. Everyone was allocated a tutor whose duty it was to keep an eye on your moral welfare, 'in loco parentis'. For me this was Dr Cameron-Wilson, a modern linguist and a rather earnest and pious man, not someone I would particularly have wanted to confide in had I needed.

The college regime in 1969 was still quite regimented. A long set of instructions were issued – a guide to undergraduate life at Jesus College, and this included a recommendation to buy a gown to the Jesus College pattern from Messrs Bodger & Co. of 47 & 48 Sidney Street, price £3 18s 6d. Dinner had to be taken every day in hall, and gowns, jackets and ties were compulsory. You also had to pay for breakfast in hall whether you ate it or not. Gowns had to be worn when seeing tutors and theoretically even at lectures. But things were changing fast. The anachronistic gate hours were in the process of being relaxed or abolished. Although the main gates shut at midnight, it was possible to pre-arrange entry with the porters up until 6 a.m., which still counted as spending the night in college (which was a strict requirement). In any event, Jesus was probably the easiest college to climb into, just a small hop over a low fence on Park Street at the back of the squash courts and hockey pitch. One did hear gory tales of less fortunate students being impaled on railings trying to get into more heavily defended colleges. Probably as an incentive to keep undergraduates in college, the bar in the Junior Common Room stayed open until midnight, an hour or more after the town pubs had shut.

The porters were a powerful brigade, definitely worth keeping on one's side, no more so than Mr E.J. West, who had been head porter since 1956. 'Fats' West, as he was known behind his back, was a stately figure, and in his top hat and morning coat he was reckoned to be the best turned-out head porter in Cambridge, and certainly an adornment to the college scene. It was a sad day when the familiar sight of Mr West standing on the landing ringing the hand bell for dinner in hall was replaced by an electric push-button bell.

The dons or Fellows were a more elusive bunch. There were legends, like Arthur Quiller Couch who had been Professor of English from 1912 to 1944, and whose former room in C4 in First Court was still known as the Qbicle, and Dr Freddie Brittain who had died in 1969 and to whom a plaque was unveiled on the east chapel wall. The Master was Sir Denys Page, a classicist, who I met only once in my three years, and even then only a polite hand shake and 'hello' at a reception. That too was the only time I saw inside the Master's Lodge. There were revered academic figures such as Charles Wilson, who had been at Jesus since 1933 and was Professor of Modern History from 1963 to 1979, the celebrated lawyer Raymond Williams and Sir Leslie Martin, chair of the school of architecture from 1956 to 1972. He was rarely seen in college, preferring to live and work in his own self-designed house and studio in a converted mill at Great Shelford.

Some Fellows went out of their way to meet and entertain undergraduates. Everyone was invited to drink sherry with the erudite Dr Ilya Gershevitch, the Persian specialist, or the sporty Reverend Peter Allen, who was chaplain, and a far more approachable man than the Dean, Peter Baelz. Dr Laurence Picken was also an excellent host, softly spoken and modest in demeanour but with an extraordinary collection of Chinese musical instruments. The most elderly Fellow was Dr Alan Pars who had been a mathematician at Jesus since 1915, and was very much part of the fixture and fittings. Rather like E.M. Forster at King's, he was one of those recluses who had few external contacts or family and had to be farmed out for Christmas when the college dining hall was closed. His hunched gait, eyes downcast, stick raised behind, was an unmistakable sight as he took his afternoon constitutional around the college. He invited select group of students to his room for a breakfast of boiled eggs and long anecdotes about pre-war Cambridge. As his obituarist tactfully put it when he died in 1985 aged eighty-nine, 'his consuming interest in people sometimes manifested itself in indiscretion or a taste for gossip'.

The college was, of course, an all-male institution, with the exception of the poorly-paid women who came in every day to clean and make beds, and Sister Brady who had been the college nurse since 1945. These were redoubtable ladies, such as Mrs Nightingale and Tilly Patten, who had both worked for over forty years when they retired in 1970. Some wrangler calculated that between them they'd made over 100,000 beds. There was huge loyalty to the college among its servants. Mr Howard, the head gardener, had started as a lad in 1925, and eventually did fifty-one years for the college. Mr Robinson had worked in the bursary and buttery since 1931; Billy Farrington had been head chef since 1939.

Apart from Girton, Newnham and New Hall, all the other Cambridge colleges in 1969 were men-only, and there was a huge imbalance between the sexes in the university. Homerton teacher training college for women on Hills Road, next to my old school, and a few language schools helped only a little to dent the ratio of ten-to-one. A few brave souls invited even braver girls into college hall for dinner, but most undergraduates hung on to their home-town girlfriends, if they had one. The idea of mixed colleges was still remote and the possibilities of women staying over strictly against the regulations. The bedders provided a prurient police force. It is said that the first woman to be allowed officially to stay overnight in college was in February 1966, and that was Mrs Muriel Brittain, who had been married to Dr Brittain since 1959! I expect others preceded her without permission.

Suffering from a degree of shyness, immaturity and inferiority, I did not get involved with any of the various societies and clubs in college. Some of these were standard hangovers from school – the chess club, debating society and sports teams – but others such as the Roosters, the Red Herrings, the Natives, the Genials and the Radegund Society were much stranger and seemingly exclusive or elitist. I never found out how you joined or were invited. The George Corrie Society existed to venerate the memory of a former Master who was violently opposed to change. Its manifesto was openly 'to counteract the influence of the left-wing members of the university who seek to pervert her noblest traditions'. I also steered clear of college chapel and its choir, which was devoted to maintaining the highest traditions of the Church of England, about which I knew or appreciated very little.

In the second year we had to find digs from an approved list of lodgings. In my first term at Chapel Court I had succeeded in purloining a battered Bechstein upright piano, allegedly left behind by Nicholas Monserrat's son, and inherited by my bassoonist friend Jo Burton, who had moved into Neville Court, Trinity. Fortunately the move caused only minor damage to the seventeenth-century staircase! Keen on finding somewhere to accommodate this honkey-tonk, I looked at a house in Chaucer Road lived in by Woodrow Wyatt's mother. It was an idyllic spot, but she admitted to being averse to music, so I opted instead for a top floor room, without piano, at No.63 Jesus Lane, one of the numerous houses there owned by the college. Even Mrs West, the head porter's wife, took in students at No.49.

Mrs Harvey ran the house at No.63, and her meek husband, with a rod of iron. Mr Harvey was rarely seen, normally kept under lock and key in the basement where they lived, except when he hoovered the stair carpet on Sunday mornings, muttering oaths under his breath, and making sure no-one could enjoy a lie-in. My room was at the back of the house looking towards King Street and the trees of Christ's Pieces, and at least it was convenient, as close to college hall and the bar as many rooms within college itself.

For the last year there was a lottery draw for rooms in college, there being space for only about half the third year undergraduates, the remainder having to find lodgings outside. I came sixth, and thus had prime pick, and chose a suite on L Staircase, comprising a living room, separate bedroom and gyp room. With no lavatory on the staircase it was also cheap – a deprivation worth suffering. Per square foot there was no better value in college.

Under the grant system Cambridge undergraduates were allowed £400 per year in 1969/70 for their food and accommodation. For some privileged reason this was the same level as London students, and higher than for other provincial universities. The money was provided by the local education authority, but means tested to assess how much parents should contribute. My father was earning £2,500 that year and had to contribute £150 towards my keep. All the tuition fees to the college and university were paid separately, essentially by the State. By 1971/72 the allowance had gone up to £465 per year, my father's salary had risen to £3,000, and he had to contribute £196. Unlike students today, I was completely shielded from any direct financial obligation, loans or debts. My first year Chapel Court room cost £90 for the year, meals in college another £80, which left plenty spare. My final year rooms were only £75, a bargain. At the end you got back the £25 'caution money' which had been deposited at the start.

In September 1971 I had bought an Erard grand piano for £5 from David Short, who was the landlord of the Queen's Head pub at Newton, and known to my then-girlfriend. I thought it would look grand in my new L Staircase living room. Sadly the Millers removal men, try as they did, could not get it round the bend in the stairs, so it sat outside in the courtyard for two weeks until I sold it for £3 to one of the porters.

L Staircase was also one of the coldest in college. In January 1971 there had been a great tragedy when a student died in his room on staircase 9 in Chapel Court, asphyxiated by carbon monoxide from a faulty and archaic gas fire. Central heating was introduced, with haste, but L Staircase, without water, was last in the phasing. Fortunately the winter of 1971/72 was not a severe one by Cambridge standards.

Barry Flanagan's 'Bronze Horse' in First Court.

My affection for the college grew each year I was there. Rules were relaxed, although we all continued to wear gowns for dinner in hall as protection from spillage of soup and custard by the waiters. Breakfast was no longer compulsorily paid for, and you could opt out of dinners. I gradually learnt that the confident bluster of the public school rowers was best ignored. I found and made friends with those of like-minds. Towards the end, I came to realise just how lucky I had been, to have had the privilege of living in such a venerable institution, albeit for just nine short terms.

Much has changed at Jesus over the last thirty-five years. In 1970 a 'new building' fund was set up, culminating in the opening in 1996 of the Quincentenary Library and Computer Centre to celebrate the 500th anniversary of the college. That too was further extended in 2001, by the same architects Evans and Shalev, to create a new residential block facing Jesus Lane, and forming a new three-side Library Court. Both these buildings are in a conservative design with pale buff brick, matching the rather dull 1930s Morley Horder block on the south side of Chapel Court. One critic described the old-fashioned staircase layout as being 'so traditional it can be considered radical in the extreme'.

In 2006 the now-listed North Court buildings of David Roberts were adapted to give each bedroom its own en-suite bathroom, with new communal kitchens in the basement. This was probably a response to client requirements for lucrative conference lettings in the vacation, on which every bursar now depends, rather than pampering the term-time students. In 2007 a new two-manual organ was installed in the chapel and a new floor laid in the hall, retaining the eighteenth-century stone flags and the even older timbers beneath.

Perhaps the most striking visual change to the college began in 1983 with a special exhibition of open-air sculpture. Its success instigated a biannual display, and the acquisition of various pieces for permanent embellishments to the grounds. Thus today there is Barry Flanagan's 'Bronze Horse' in First Court, and works by Anthony Gormley, Eduardo Paolozzi, Richard Long and many others. These have put Jesus firmly on the visitor map.

In 1974, following more progressive colleges such as King's, Clare and Churchill, the decision was taken to admit women, the first Fellow in 1976 and then undergraduates in 1979. By 1987 one-third were women. In 1984 Prince Edward was admitted as a freshman, and his mum and dad paid him, and the college, a visit, amid some pomp.

Masters have come and gone: Alan Cottrell, Colin Renfrew, David Crighton, who died young, and now Robert Mair. He was brought up in Cambridge, went to the Leys School, and knew my mother from church. His appointment as Master coincided with a drive to improve access to the college for students from state schools.

Most of the Fellows who I remember from forty years ago have died, most recently Alan Sharpe. Peter Glazebrook has edited a comprehensive history of Jesus College. I have returned, infrequently, to reunion dinners, in 1980 and 1988, and taken the chance to see how some of your contemporaries have aged and what sort of corporate cars and jobs they have. More happily I have occasionally walked around the beautiful grounds with friends who've been visiting Cambridge or on my own.

In 1970 we crammed into a tiny TV room to watch in black and white the World Cup from Mexico and the Ali-Frazier fight. Now there are flat screens in the bar, students have televisions in their rooms; computers and lap-tops are universal. Technology moves on, but not always the issues. The Dean of St John's recently set up a Facebook profile under an assumed name to spy on a protest group complaining about drinking restrictions in hall.

And yet, as Lord Adrian, sometime Master of Trinity, once said: 'The time may come when the colleges may become alms-houses for the old and cafeterias for the young, but it will always be something to have fallen asleep to the sound of the fountain playing in Trinity Great Court'.

So with Jesus there is the wisteria in First Court, the mellow red brickwork in the afternoon sun, the autumn leaves blown from the mighty trees in the Fellows' Garden, the sound of unseen footsteps in Cloister Court, things eternal which alumni remember and the young will continue to enjoy.

It was King James I who allegedly said that 'were he to choose, he would pray at King's, dine at Trinity, and study and sleep at Jesus'. That would still be a good choice.

## UNIVERSITY FACULTY

In my year's intake at Jesus College there were only a handful of us reading Geography. In any event, all the teaching was organised and provided by the faculty, not by the college. Despite having Bruce Sparks as my Director of Studies in my first year, I never had him for supervision. For that I went to Barbara Kennedy at New Hall. The lectures were all held in the Department of Geography at the far end of Downing Place, part of the large Downing site, rather dreary and functional.

Having done no Mathematics since O-Level I found the Geography syllabus an almighty shock, dominated as it was by statistics. My A-Level Geography had given me no adequate preparation for the traumas which lay ahead. Thus I was plunged lock-stock-and barrel into systems theory, models, spatial systems, probability versus determinism, auto-correlation, regression, nomothetic exceptionalism, idiography, predictive diffusion and all sorts of other jargon and gobbledy-gook. Perhaps I would understand it better now, but at the time even such concepts as entropy (the amount of 'organisation' or 'randomness' in a system), game theory and paradigms left me floundering.

The lectures of Richard Chorley, who had written seminal 'must-read' text books, were the most frustrating. He was clearly a brilliant man and sometimes highly amusing with his west-country twang, but his discourse was shrouded in an impenetrable fog of binomial equations, frequency distributions and Kolmogorov-Smirnov tests. Barbara Kennedy, to whom I had to submit essays and endure an intellectual grilling during supervisions, was equally besotted with mathematics.

University of Cambridge, Department of Geography, Downing Place.

The lectures of Bruce Sparks where he talked about the local geology and erosion of East Anglia and such local and familiar phenomena as the 'Harston gorge', were more understandable, but I was gradually drawn to the more approachable and ultimately more interesting aspects of human and economic geography. H.C. Darby was the professor, by then a grand old man and author of the great pre-war books *Domesday England* and *The Draining of the Fens*, but he didn't appear much and was regarded with some disdain by the young statistical whiz-kids. For my Part II I specialised in economics, geographical philosophy, Latin America and applied Geography, which mercifully involved little statistics. By now I had left Bruce Sparks and his soil erosion and Barbara Kennedy with her quantitative analysis far behind. In my college Dr Robin Donkin, who specialised in historical and Latin America, took over as my Director of Studies, issuing hugely long reading lists and demanding high standards of essay writing, but at least it was on subjects that I understood. I now had tutorials and seminars with Dr Tess Adkins, who was a recently elected Fellow at enlightened King's and a great delight. She was married to John Adkins, a physicist Fellow at Jesus who I knew as an enthusiastic amateur oboist, and they lived in a college-owned house in Park Terrace, the largest and best late Georgian domestic terrace in Cambridge. Supervisions in the splendour of their first floor front room, looking out across Parker's Piece, were a joy, usually enhanced by a pleasant tipple of John's homemade beer.

Fortunately for me, continuous assessment was not a major part of the regime at that time, as it tends to be today, and all the examinations came in a clump at the end of the summer or Easter term, which suited me. These were held mainly in the Scott Polar Research Institute in Lensfield Road, and the last year Finals involved six three-hour exams sat on five consecutive days at the end of May. There was also a dissertation, essentially a long essay on a supposedly original subject, handed in at the beginning of that term, in which I analysed the different

Degree Day, June 1972. (Author's Collection)

types of agriculture in several villages around Cambridge, where topography, land ownership and soil fertility resulted in marked variations – nothing very earth shattering. What a relief when it was all over! The results were out within a few days, blurred in a haze of celebration and exhaustion.

Degree day was on Saturday 24 June, after all the festivities had finished. This was organised by college, not by subject or faculty. Special gowns with white ermine trim had to be hired, once again from Bodgers, and having assembled at Jesus we processed in orderly fashion from First Court through the gatehouse, down the Chimney, along Jesus Lane and Trinity Street to the Senate House to hear a lot of Latin and to collect a Batchelor of Arts degree. Outside on the immaculate lawns were proud parents, my father in his best Sunday suit taking photographs, my mother wearing her smartest hat. This was a chance to walk on the most cossetted piece of turf in Cambridge, rolled and cut, rolled and cut, for 300 years. During the war someone had suggested to Winston Churchill that it should be used to grow vegetables; 'it is for lawns like these that we are fighting' he replied. In May 1976, having taken no further exam other than existing for the minimum number of ten terms, staying out of prison, and paying £10 for the privilege, I returned to collect my Master of Arts.

After leaving, and going perhaps predictably into town planning, I didn't keep up with my tutors or teachers. Bruce Sparks, who gave me my first chance, retired in 1982 and died six years later. Richard Chorley who took over from Darby as Head of the Geography Department in 1972 died in 2002. Robin Donkin died in 2006.

Looking back at the academic experience as an undergraduate at Cambridge it was if nothing else a chance to learn how to work on your own. The intellectual challenge stretched the mind and probably pushed the brain in certain directions. Compared to the poor medics and scientists who had hours of laboratory experiments every day as well as their lectures and supervisions, my course was not very hard work. Once I understood what I was studying, I learnt which lectures to avoid and which supervisors to respect.

Above all it gave me time, in those ludicrously short terms, to do lots of other things.

# EXTRA MURAL ACTIVITIES

While I found it difficult or unworthwhile to integrate into the organised social life and establishment community of Jesus College I was unusually lucky in that I already knew plenty of people at other colleges. This was almost entirely a result of the National Youth Orchestra which I'd been in for the whole of 1968/69, and from which a clutch of us were starting together at Cambridge. It was an instant cross-college clique, and an entrance into high-quality university music which I would never otherwise have had.

In the first week of term there was a 'Freshers Fair', held in the shabby old Corn Exchange where all the university societies laid out their stalls and tried to entice new members. There were endless drinks parties at which it was easy to get outrageously drunk on free college sherry or a lethal punch concoction. In an inebriated state I signed up for life membership of the Geographical Society.

I also joined the Cambridge University Music Society (CUMS), which ran two orchestras and a choir, and the Cambridge University Music Club which ran a series of Saturday evening chamber concerts in the Music School and a newly formed chamber orchestra, for both of which I was immediately auditioned.

I got into the first orchestra of CUMS. This was a long established and very efficiently run organisation, and I soon came into contact with the redoubtable secretary Irene Seccombe. Rehearsals were held every Tuesday evening in the Music School in Downing Place, starting at 8.15 p.m. after college hall and finishing at 10.15 p.m., giving plenty of time for beer. Ms Seccombe would be there, just inside the pale blue street door, spectacles perched on the end of her nose, busily ticking off names as you went in, or ticking you off if you were late.

More importantly CUMS was my first introduction to David Willcocks, who conducted the choir and orchestra. As a child I'd seen him from afar in King's Chapel; now I met him close-up. He was dapper and diminutive, yet a commanding figure with ever-twinkling eyes, a ready smile and a quick breezy walk. As indeed everybody said, he was a lovely, easy-going man, but also a brilliant musician, equally demanding and understanding, doing his utmost to get the best out of everyone in the room, 'Fourth horn', he might say, 'yes, that bottom F, a difficult note, a little flat I think, yes, a difficult note, good, good…'

In my first term we did Janacek's *Glagolitic Mass*, performed in King's College Chapel on the last Thursday of term, with Jane Manning, Alfreda Hodgson and John Mitchinson as fantastic soloists, and the mighty organ stretched to its limits in the thunderous finale. In the summer May Week concert it was the turn of Walton's *Belshazzar's Feast*, and the following summer Elgar's *Dream of Gerontius*. For this we had the rare privilege of being directed by Benjamin Britten, who was conducting the work for the first time, alongside Peter Pears and Benjamin Luxon. It was a tradition to repeat the May Week concert a few days later at the Snape Maltings in Suffolk, hence the Britten/Pears connection. I had missed the drama of June 1969 when the old Maltings had burnt down the night before the concert, which was relocated with some improvisation to Blythburgh church. June 1971 was a celebration of the re-opening.

For all his fame Britten's conducting was lacklustre compared to Willcocks, and it made us realise, much though many mimicked him, how lucky we were. Willcocks had started conducting CUMS in 1957 when he'd come to be Director of Music at King's as successor to Boris Ord. For the three years I was in CUMS, Willcocks was in his prime, soon to move on to become Director of the Royal College of Music in 1974, and to be knighted in 1977. I was lucky to catch him, and it is wonderful that he is, at eighty-nine, still going strong.

I was even luckier to be enlisted by him to partake in King's College choir performances in the Chapel when they needed instrumental players to augment the organ. A Bach cantata might form part of the Sunday morning service, or Fauré's *Requiem* on Remembrance Day. On the first Sunday after Ascension we played Handel's *Chandos Anthems*, and in March 1970 the *St John Passion* with choral scholars past and present taking the solo parts. These were memorable occasions, put together with minimum rehearsal and great deftness under David Willcocks' baton. We each got an 'honorarium' of £1, which was quite handsome. Often on Sunday mornings much was sight-read, once with a bleary-eyed trumpeter, hastily summoned, still wearing his pyjamas under his coat.

It was customary for the CUMS orchestral concert in February to be conducted, at least in part, by a student 'assistant', alongside Willcocks. In 1970 this was Antony Beaumont, a talented violinist and budding musicologist, who subsequently made his career in Germany, and in 1972 it was Nicholas McGegan, who went on to excel as a baroque flaustist and now conducts mainly in the USA. Richard Hickox, late much lamented, who was organ scholar at Queens', only got to conduct the Gilbert and Sullivan Society.

Antony Beaumont and Dave Dennis, who I'd known in the NYO, auditioned me for the student-run Music Club orchestra, CUMC, and I was fortunate enough to take part in the concert in the Guildhall when the elderly David Oistrakh played the Beethoven *Violin Concerto*, one of his last performances in England. More hastily put together were the Saturday night chamber concerts held in the University Music School, each one organised by a couple of students from the committee. Somehow I was selected or volunteered to play in the shop-window Freshmen's Concert, alongside various other pals from the NYO. In the other concerts, budding impresarios vied with each other to stage the most imaginative or off-the-wall programmes, with mixed end results. There were entertaining post-concert parties, such as when the cellist Naomi Butterworth played Saint-Saens' *Swan* with a grapefruit or 'chord jousting' when David Willcocks would challenge all-comers on the two pianos.

It was easy to get sucked into a huge amount of music making. At Jesus, college music was heavily based around the chapel where Terry Allbright was a competent organist and pianist and a dominant force. All the other colleges had music societies which put on concerts, sometimes requiring orchestras or choirs, and I was soon involved in a merry-go-round of concerts, dragooned in as a 'ringer'. Such was the advantage and easy temptation of being a bassoonist in short supply.

Everything culminated in May Week, a flurry of activity when dozens of concerts, operas, plays with incidental music and sundry entertainments were crammed into the first two weeks of June. Some people managed to play in more than one concert in an evening, racing from one venue to another, perhaps a first half in Emmanuel and a second half in Trinity. The King's May Week concerts were the most sumptuous, with extensive interval refreshments to lubricate the second half. Philip Radcliffe, the eccentric music Fellow at King's, was always in his pomp.

At the time all this was exciting and enervating. Most of the concerts were probably not as good as many of the performers thought they were, but for sheer exposure to new pieces, the sharpening of one's sight-reading skills and the social intercourse, there was no equal. I wonder now, when each term was only eight weeks long, how there was time to do any work, as well as play squash, perfect one's punting skills on the river, or drink with friends in the college bars and pubs.

Many happy hours were spent in Corpus where I had a group of friends and made others. In this tiny college, the benevolent and liberal influence of Richard Bainbridge, the senior tutor, was clearly apparent, and the austerity of the décor of the college bar was compensated by the facilities for table-football. The bar at Trinity where I socialised with Jo Burton was the opposite, as snug and comfortable as a Home Counties country pub. Corpus however had Leckhampton, its graduate hostel off Grange Road where the secluded grounds and the swimming pool provided a fabulous venue for some wild parties.

In my first year at college I also carried on playing in the Cambridge Philharmonic Orchestra. After Denis Fielder's departure the baton had been handed on to charismatic and charming Hugh MacDonald, a young academic and Berlioz expert, and married to the beautiful Naomi Butterworth. Bernard Blay, Arnold Ashby and Anne Macnaghten, who had for many years led the string sections for Denis, moved to Hitchin. Paul Collins, a gruff Canadian who knew my uncle John from his Hampstead drinking haunts came to lead the orchestra. In January 1970 he and Naomi played the Brahms 'double' and we did *Peter and the Wolf* with David Willcocks narrating. That turned out to be my final Philharmonic concert. By then I had been invited to join the East Anglian Student Orchestra which was much superior, and as good as the National Youth Orchestra which I'd also had to leave having reached their age limit. That final NYO concert, also in January 1970, with Pierre Boulez conducting *The Rite of Spring* and *La Mer* was a landmark too.

The East Anglian Student Orchestra was run and financed by a Bury St Edmunds businessman, David Simpson, with the laudable aim of bringing together the best of the region's amateur and professional students aged seventeen to twenty-five for weekend rehearsals and concerts, under the dynamic conducting of Graham Treacher. My first concert with them was in the Cambridge Guildhall in March 1970, performing *Daphnis and Chloe* and Tchaikovsky's *Fourth Symphony*, repeated in Bedford and Lavenham. I continued to play regularly with EASO until it folded in 1976, much lamented.

I also carried on playing sporadically in George Barker's Uttlesforde Orchestra. In October 1970 we played at a 'Viennese Assembly' hosted by the Nevilles at Audley End, near Saffron Walden, where the drink at the ready disposal of the players resulted in some rather loose renditions of Strauss waltzes. There was also ad hoc chamber music with John Adkins and Nick Shackleton, both brilliant academics in their own fields and enthusiastic amateur woodwind players. Nick lived in Claremont with his wife Judith and Chris Hogwood, the same house I had visited as a boy when the Sharpes were there. Now, instead of model trains, it was stuffed with basset horns and serpents.

Throughout my three years as an undergraduate I kept the same girlfriend I'd known from school. She was studying at the Guildhall School of Music in London, at that time still in their creaking old premises in John Carpenter Street in the back streets behind Fleet Street and the Embankment. Journeys to London were done by hitch-hiking, not a fashionable activity today, but surprisingly easy then. The first stretch of Trumpington Road, after the junction with Fen Causeway opposite the Leys School, was a sure-fire place to catch a ride. All long-distance traffic was still, pre-bypass, grinding round the Backs or through the centre of town. Hitching back to Cambridge was less straightforward, but I usually took the No. 113 Routemaster bus to Hendon or Apex Corner and rarely had to wait more than ten minutes. People were more generous and less suspicious than today.

Through music I had, as a performer, been to many May Balls, once three on consecutive nights, where usually the 'fee' for playing various sets of background music was free food and drink, and the opportunity to enjoy the fun of the fair. Only in my last term did I buy a ticket at the stiff price of £25 for two for the Jesus May Ball. It was an extravagant affair, unlimited champagne, luxurious food, huge marquees in Chapel Court and Pump Court, everybody dressed in their finest evening wear, girls summoned or cajoled to attend by their men from all parts of the country. There was competition among the colleges to hire the best bands, such as The Who, Led Zeppelin, even the Rolling Stones. The Jesus Ball boasted Public Foot The Roman, East of Eden, Ravin' Rupert and the Leaping Armadillo Sisters, not that they meant much to me. I preferred the Milne MacDonald Big Band.

At 4 a.m. and the first light of dawn the ticket obtained entry to Corpus, Emmanuel and other colleges which were also holding their May Balls that night. From St Catharine's I had arranged with friends to take a punt up the river to Grantchester meadows, and there, with the sun burning away the early mist, we had a picnic breakfast on the dewy grass. It was as romantic an end to an unreal way of life as one could have hoped for.

Ahead lay another and more serious world, returning to the parental home or finding a job.

## PUBS

My parents didn't go to pubs. For my mother they represented places where men went to escape from an overcrowded or unhappy household, to evade domestic chores, and to waste the weekly wage. Probably in the 1950s there were still many pubs in the poorer parts of Cambridge town which served that very purpose. Our nearest pubs in Histon Road, The Grapes and The British Queen seemed to fit that image, although I never went inside, or even saw through the frosted glass in the windows. My father was perfectly content relaxing with his family, listening to his favourite radio programmes, reading the *Daily Telegraph* or gardening. With a social life based around the non-conformist church, and a protestant work-ethic at his office, he had no drinking companions to lure him away from hearth and home. Even tea shops such as the Dorothy café, the Whim in Trinity Street and the Copper Kettle in Kings Parade were shunned by my mother. She always thought that she could make a better cuppa at home.

Discovering pubs, in all their different guises and various charms, was part of my adolescent reaction against my parents' habits, and fully in line with the laddish behaviour of my contemporaries at school and the Tech. Going to the pub was something you had to do to be 'in' with the crowd, even if you had, as in my case, precious little spending money.

At school there were sixth-formers who went to the Earl of Derby, a simple brick structure immediately across the Hills Road railway bridge, at that time grubby with the adjacent steam engine smoke, and still dowdy judging by some reports. The teachers preferred the Osborne

The Cricketers, Melbourne Place.

The Free Press, Prospect Row.

The Queen's Head, Newton.                    The Blue Ball, Grantchester.

Arms on the other side, slightly closer to the War Memorial roundabout with Station Road, and marginally less grotty according to a brave boy who once dared to venture inside.

When I started hanging out at the Tech. in Bradmore Street, I was introduced to a clutch of tiny back-street pubs on the other side of East Road. Three pubs were remarkably close together, The Free Press in Prospect Row, The Cricketers in Melbourne Place and The Elm Tree on the junction with the top of Orchard Street, all within a hundred yards of each other as indeed they still are today. This network of narrow streets and passages was the south part of the area known as the Kite which was blighted with threats of redevelopment and very run-down as a result. There was talk of the whole area being cleared, right through to Parker's Piece. At that time the Elm Tree had a French landlady, which gave the simple interior a rather exotic air, especially when she played Edith Piaf songs on the gramophone and smoked her gauloise. Sadly the interior was gutted by fire a few years later, but the building was restored and re-opened, and it now has jazz evenings. The pretty back-streets were reprieved from redevelopment, and gentrified.

Largely because of its proximity to the Perse Girls' school, the Panton Arms also became a favourite haunt for some, with a landlady who turned a mature blind eye to under-age customers and time-keeping. The Spread Eagle on Lensfield Road (now oddly renamed the Snug) and the Alma in Russell Terrace were distinctly unfriendly by comparison. The nearby Martin's coffee house at the top end of Trumpington Street was a more discreet place, where I did my first courting, and is little changed after forty years.

In the centre of Cambridge itself the pubs were dominated in term-time by undergraduates. The Pickerel in Bridge Street was to all intents and purposes the Magdalene College bar, and the Baron of Beef and The Mitre towards the Round Church were equally popular with John's men. I particularly liked the atmosphere in the Mitre, at that time under Ind Coope ownership with a jolly landlord and a hugely amiable and long-suffering St Bernard dog.

By the time I became an undergraduate, Jesus College acting as landowner and developer was doing its best to destroy the famous King Street run. This quaint street once had a dozen pubs. Even in 1953 there were still six, the Cambridge Arms, the Earl Grey, the Champion of the Thames, the Horse and Groom, the Radegund and the Royal Arms, and a pint in each was still a challenging race, so much so that the Proctors banned it in 1964. By 1969 there were only four pubs left, although the Corner House café was still on the corner with Malcolm Street, the best 'greasy spoon' in Cambridge. Happily the Champion of the Thames, with its draught beers served 'from the wood' from the barrels propped up behind the bar, and the Radegund, Cambridge's smallest pub still survive. The dear old Corner House has gone, replaced by a bland 1970s scheme which includes a restaurant/ bar called the Bun Shop. The Horse and Groom has now been renamed the King Street Run.

The original Bun Shop was the nearest pub to the Music School and Geography Department in Downing Place, just across Downing Street in St Tibbs Row, and at certain times, notably after CUMS rehearsals, the most crowded pub in town. Despite its disrepair it was probably an eighteenth-century building, maybe even earlier beneath its skin, and preposterously was demolished to make way for the Lion Yard scheme. Somehow the dingy Victorian Red Cow with its torn and tatty seats and rough clientele was spared, and it has now been revamped as The Cow.

With the demise of the King Street run, hardy souls with greater stamina attempted similar exploits along the Newmarket Road. Between Four Lamps roundabout and the airport there were nearly twenty pubs, and not many gems. Few got beyond The Wrestlers, The Bird in Hand and The Zebra on Maids Causeway, and there were tempting sideways distractions with The Hopbine in Fair Street and The Ancient Druids (now The Box Tree) in Napier Street.

Several of Cambridge's most historic pubs have changed out of recognition. The Eagle in Bene't Street was a welcome relief from the severity and noise of Corpus bar, but in the 1980s it was ruined by a huge sprawling extension. The so-called RAF room has been preserved, with the wartime squadron numbers singed onto the ceiling, but it is now a mega-pub, swamped with rubber-necking tourists wanting to see where in 1953 Crick and Watson, during a lunchtime break from the old Cavendish laboratories, announced their discovery of 'the secret of life', or DNA. The former Bath Hotel next door is now a better bet.

The Fountain in Regent Street used to be one of the roughest central pubs, where town skinheads or rockers sometimes congregated, looking for trouble, but has now been modernised and sanitised out of recognition. The Blue Boar in Trinity Street, once the smartest bar in Cambridge, has been repeatedly re-hashed, and the drinking bit is now called the Bar Ha Ha and the eating bit the Strada. The Turk's Head, almost next door, became a Berni Inn, and a respectable retreat for parents visiting their student offspring. The Little Rose opposite Peterhouse was transformed into a Loch Fyne seafood restaurant; nothing remains of the Rose Tavern in Rose Crescent.

Riverside pubs were always a good summer-time destination. The Fort St George, opposite the boat houses on Jesus Green, was well frequented by the hearty Jesus rowing brigade, and best avoided by the timid. The Pike and Eel further downstream had more normal customers, and is still one of the best places to watch the skullers and eights skimming past. The once-idyllic Plough at Fen Ditton has been wrecked; with its enormous car parks and conservatory extensions it is more like a motorway service station than a country pub.

The Anchor by Silver Street bridge used to attract the language school girls, but served stale beer at high prices. A 'W' was often daubed in front of the sign. The Mill was better and with a more pleasant outside space to watch the water rushing over the weir and laugh at the inexperienced punters struggling with the currents. The Granta was a quieter and more charming spot beside the Mill Pool at Newnham, approached by punt down the muddy backwater behind Darwin College, but that too was grossly extended. Ludovick Stewart was a constant regular there, staggering across the road from the Maltings, and would not have been amused to see it now.

When there was access to a car the delights of country pubs in the surrounding villages could be enjoyed. The Queen's Head at Newton was everyone's favourite, with delicious Adnams beer from Southwold, bare scrubbed tables, skittles in the public bar and the simplest food of soup served with great hunks of bread. The Tickell Arms in nearby Whittlesford was more of an acquired taste, run by the eccentric Kim Tickell. In this blue-painted Gothic dolls-house there was Wagner blaring from the speakers, pretty blond German boys serving behind the bar, and Kim presiding over the gaiety, insisting that ties and jackets be worn by all the men, and occasionally making politically incorrect remarks. He also produced excellent food, at a time when most pubs offered only peanuts and perhaps a scotch egg. One of those was the Three Horseshoes at Madingley, hard to believe today when it is heralded as one of the best gastropubs in England, according to a recent review in the *Guardian*.

Few country or suburban pubs can survive today without serving food. The Slap Up Inn at Waterbeach is now the Slap Up Tandoori, The Volunteer at Trumpington is the Spice Merchant, while The Travellers Rest on the Huntingdon Road is a sprawling Beefeater. One exception, which deserves to be preserved forever, along with its landlord, is the Blue Ball in Grantchester, surely one of the least spoilt pubs in the county.

As a student I was weaned on nasty new keg beers such as Double Diamond, McEwans Export and Watneys Red Barrel; the college bars sold little else. Aided and abetted by my friends I did find and acquire a taste for good draught beer. Tolly Cobbold, Charles Wells, Greene King, Ruddles and Adnams were available, but lots of pubs sold only fizzy keg or were in the process of getting rid of their traditional hand pumps. In 1971 the national Campaign for Real Ale was founded (in St Albans), just in the nick of time to stem the evil tide.

# JOBS

Employment opportunities in Cambridge in the 1950s and '60s were restricted to a few distinct sectors. The university dominated the town, not only the academic staff who generally lived within the confines of college or in the smarter west or south side of Cambridge, but many hundreds of porters, cooks, bed-makers, gardeners, cleaners and other college servants who mainly lived in the poorer east and northern parts of town.

The shops and service trades, as in any provincial market town, provided a living for many, together with the usual professions of solicitors, doctors, dentists, school teachers and estate agents. There were the City and County Councils in the Guildhall and County Hall at the top of Castle Hill. My father was part of the Cambridge-based regional government, congregated in the side roads off Brooklands Avenue.

The small amount of industry which existed was highly specialised. W.G. Pye started out making scientific instruments for the Cavendish Laboratories but then expanded into wider electrical goods in their Granta Works in Chesterton. Pye Telecommunications Ltd flourished in the 1950s and '60s, and employed hundreds of skilled workers, until they were taken over by Phillips in 1976 and undone by Far East competition. Cambridge Consultants had been founded in 1960, 'to put the brains of Cambridge University at the disposal of the problems of British industry'.

Out on the Harston Road was Fison Agrochemicals plant where they made pesticides and fertilisers, and ruined the setting of the once picturesque Hauxton Mill next door. CIBA had a similar factory out at Duxford. At Barrington there were the cement works. The only industry which offered opportunities for unskilled or casual work was Chivers Jam factory in Histon.

As a schoolboy I'd made-do on my menial pocket money and avoided the chore of doing early morning paper rounds or working in shops on Saturdays, which many of my friends had to do. As a student all that changed. My parents gave me no extra money other than my term-time grant, so of necessity the job market beckoned.

In the three or four weeks before Christmas the General Post Office was a popular choice for temporary work and the plum daytime jobs were difficult to get. I was allocated early morning parcel sorting, which meant getting up horribly early to arrive for 6.00 a.m. at the former drill hall behind the Mill Road office (where Petersfield Mansions now stands). Our task was to unload the sacks delivered by vans from the station and place the parcels into the large wicker trolleys which filled the hall, each labelled for different villages and districts of town. It has to be said that each parcel was not always handled with loving care, and an accurate throw was highly prized. The four regular staff left the casuals to do the work and sat in the fug of a smoke-filled room, playing cards or drinking the bounty of any bottle which had 'accidentally leaked'. In 1969 the pay was 3s 6d per hour which with an eight-hour shift, six days a week, was a tidy sum. In my third year I was promoted to rural parcel deliveries, accompanying the driver around outlying villages, opening gates, running the gauntlet of dangerous dogs and eating a vast number of mince pies. On Sundays we got double time.

In the long summer holidays which stretched from mid-June to the end of September, Chivers was the nearest and best bet to earn some money. For a while fruit picking was all I could get, on the farms and orchards which surrounded Histon, Girton and Oakington. It was gruelling and back-breaking work, especially strawberries, gooseberries and blackcurrants, and rewarded piece-work by the weight you picked. Most of the other labourers were travellers or ex-prisoners, mainly surly and unfriendly who seemed to gather twice as much as me. When I tried to copy their tricks by filling the bottom of a pallet with fallen fruit, hidden with good ones on top, I was quickly found out by the inspector. I hated it.

I was very grateful when the following summer our neighbours Claud and Cyril Maskell landed me a job in the Chivers factory itself. For 5s an hour I joined the gang in the blackcurrant jelly section, where we unloaded the lorries and poured the fruit into a huge vat where it was boiled. We then siphoned the hot juice into ten-gallon wooden barrels, hammered in the spigots and rolled them into an open yard at the back of the factory to cool down and mature. Our foreman, Gary, was a hugely obese man, probably younger than he looked. He encouraged us to take it in turns to arrive early or stay late to dock everybody's time cards on the clocking-in machine. We made him stand every morning on the weigh bridge to check that he was still over twenty stone. He showed us his girly magazines. As for the blackcurrants, Gary was in charge of adding the pectin and preservatives, and one day in a fit of pique chucked in an old pair of wellington boots, which would have added an extra jelling agent for that particular batch. I never went into the bottling or labelling sheds to find out how the sludge we put into the barrels turned into the stuff you bought in jars. Perhaps it is just as well.

Having finished at university the chances of landing a job in or near Cambridge were remote and unappealing to me at the time, and I had no desire to carry on with post-graduate studies. All my friends were off to London, whose streets were apparently paved with gold, so there I went too.

## A CHANGING TOWN

Although I now worked in London, I kept a close eye on Cambridge, and retained good friends, the parental home and many musical contacts.

The 1970s saw many radical changes to the town, much of which probably deservedly gets a bad press today. In its defence, it was a decade of transition, when the juggernaut of comprehensive redevelopment and the arrogance of modernism were challenged, and new approaches, such as conservation, became possible.

First, however, the centre of Cambridge had to suffer the atrocity that was the Lion Yard shopping centre. This involved the demolition of the whole south side of Petty Cury, including the alleys and courtyards behind, right up to Downing Street and the beloved Bun Shop. Alexander Street, Falcon Yard, St Andrew's Court with its old cottages, St Andrews Hill and St Tibb's Row were swept away. The shabby premises of the Footlights Club disappeared; so too the Hang Chow restaurant. Even the first-floor Eros restaurant on the north side of Petty Cury closed. This had been a favourite student haunt, with its college crests around the walls, much frequented for its cheap moussaka, rice and chips. When it opened in 1975 the Lion Yard and its huge multi-storey car park was a typical shopping mall; some people liked the newly pedestrianised Petty Cury and the standardised retail outlets, but a great hole had been torn through an historic area, displacing and closing many small businesses in the process. The Central Library was moved there from Wheeler Street, leaving the old library to become a tourist information office. The Corn Exchange was kept and renovated, having previously been a very run-down venue for boxing matches, the Freshers' Fair and the Beer Festival. Less forgivably a ghastly neo-Georgian Crown Plaza hotel was built fronting on to Downing Street.

The so-called Kite development was even more controversial. The land here was owned by Jesus College, who were the largest land-owner in Cambridge, at one time owning about a quarter of the town. Already in the late 1960s they had redeveloped the north side of King Street and Malcolm Place, driving a new road through to Jesus Lane, as well as office blocks such as Jupiter House in Station Road. The redevelopment potential of the Fitzroy/Burleigh Street area to swell the coffers provoked bullish reports in the Jesus College magazine, chastising the local council for indecision. Fortunately their worst ambitions were not realised, apart from the Grafton Centre, and most of the charming residential streets, including New Square and Orchard Street were saved.

Neither the Grafton Centre nor the Lion Yard provided very long-term solutions to Cambridge's shopping aspirations. Most of the Lion Yard has now been demolished and incorporated into the new Grand Arcade, opened in 2007. While the big John Lewis provides the 'anchor' store, replacing the old Robert Sayle's, there are dozens of glitzy chain shops, on three storeys, and yet another new library. Above this, inexplicably, are six levels of parking for over 900 cars. The open roof top affords an incredible panorama over the whole of central Cambridge, but conversely there are less exciting views of the car park itself from street level. No doubt intense pressure was put on the planners and Council committees by the developers and their agents to allow car parking, but that is no justification for perpetuating traffic gridlock on Cambridge's narrow streets. Corporate commercialisation is everywhere; even the Pitt Club in Jesus Lane is now a Pizza Express.

Traffic remains a major problem. The park-and-ride scheme has only been a partial success, and too many cars, encouraged by parking opportunities, still drive into the centre. The closure of King's Parade, Trinity Street, Bridge Street and Silver Street has helped, although wandering pedestrians, particularly tourists, now pose an even greater hazard to cyclists. With the increase in traffic, cycling on the main roads has become more dangerous, symbolised by the tragic death in March 2001 of John Rutter's son Christopher, on Queens' Road at the Garret Hostel Lane junction. Instead of banning cars altogether, the Council has simply made car journeys more circuitous. It was recently noted that to drive from the front of the Guildhall to the back, a distance of 200 metres by foot, takes three miles by car, thanks to the one-way system.

Public transport leaves much to be desired, and because of the dispersed nature of new employment and new housing, does not provide a realistic alternative to the car. At last the much heralded guided bus is going ahead, re-using the old disused railway line from St Ives into Cambridge, and is in an advanced stage of construction. This passes though Histon (keeping most of the old station but not the platforms), the new science park at Kings Hedges and

Milton into the city centre. It might link up with the main line station and the Trumpington park-and-ride. Perhaps it could also serve Addenbrooke's Hospital, where the paucity of public transport has resulted in massive car parking, and a hefty windfall from the charges.

The distance of the railway from the centre has always been a talking point, 'banished' as it was by the nineteenth-century dons. Improvements to the station too have been long-awaited, inevitably ensnared in the controversy of 'enabling' private development, a small part of whose profits are expected pay for works to the infrastructure. After one over-greedy scheme was rejected, another has now been approved, designed by Richard Rogers. It should provide a better concourse, bicycle parking and interchange with buses, but also proposes over 600 car parking places, surely a mistake.

Perhaps the biggest change of all in the character and role of Cambridge over the last thirty years has been the growth of commuting to London. The electrification of the Kings Cross line, which used to be slower even than the old diesel trains into Liverpool Street, coupled with the perceived quality of life. has turned Cambridge and its hinterland into a London dormitory. The attractiveness of Cambridge as 'a nice place to live' caused property prices to rocket to smart-London levels. The demand for new housing appeared insatiable.

Much of this growth, after the completion of New Chesterton and the Arbury/Kings Hedges estate, has been in the villages. Those which were allocated village colleges before the war, such as Sawston, Bottisham, Linton, Comberton and Impington/Histon were planned long ago to become mini-towns and have become as such. In 1964 a further new 'village' was proposed at Bar Hill, five miles north-west along the Huntingdon Road. In the boom years of the early 1970s and mid-1980s Bar Hill expanded at over 200 new houses per year. In 1977 a Tesco supermarket replaced the village shop, and when it was rebuilt again in 2001 it was for a few weeks the largest superstore in the country. So much for keeping things local! The new giant Waitrose at Trumpington has also added to the confused picture of car-driven shopping in Cambridge.

Whatever its faults Bar Hill has been the model for others. Cambourne, nine miles west of Cambridge on the road to Bedford, was started in 1998, aiming to provide over 3,000 new houses and a business park. The idealistic vision of it being a self-contained community, or a 'country idyll with urban amenities', is nonsense of course, simply estate agents' hype. The reality is car-dependence and a lot of travelling.

Planners have, with good reason, concentrated on what are called 'brown-field sites', that is land which has been used already for something other than farming or forestry. The old war-time airfields have been the obvious targets, notably the old Oakington airbase, which for many years was used as a refugee holding centre. When building starts in 2010 on 9,500 new houses the intention is to create an eco-town, linked to Cambridge by the guided bus, and less car dependent. Marshalls airport, largely redundant now that Stansted has taken over as the regional airport, is also a candidate for massive house building, and a possible location for a new community stadium which would accommodate Cambridge United and City football clubs and the city's rugby team.

The Holford-Wright Plan for the city of Cambridge in 1950 envisaged a total population of 86,000, including students. By 2004 it had reached 110,000, predicted to rise to 140,000 by 2020. With an additional target of 47,500 new homes in the Cambridge sub-region, there's a lot more in the pipeline. The approval of Trumpington Meadows in March 2008 is just one of several schemes on the southern fringe of Cambridge which include Glebe Farm, Clay Farm and the site of the old Bell School of languages – 4,000 houses in total. Another 'eco-town', whimsically named Hanley Grange, has been proposed ten miles south by developers, not the planners. Coping with such pressure for growth will continue to be a great challenge, even with a looming recession.

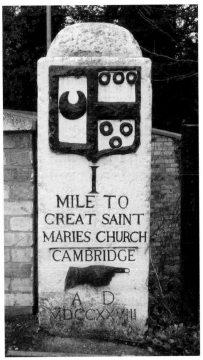

*Above:* Old-style signpost at Shelford.

*Right:* Milestone on Trumpington Road.

The countryside immediately around Cambridge has suffered the consequences, perhaps because few areas were regarded as being of outstanding natural beauty. Every village has seen some expansion, on the edges or infilling gaps. Ancient woodland and remains of ridge and furrow pasture, such as survives above Madingley, is rare around Cambridge, where almost everything has been ploughed at some time. Farmers continued to remove hedges and copses long into the 1970s and '80s, all in the name of efficiency and mechanisation. Many of the orchards and soft fruit farms have been replaced with polytunnels or oil seed rape. Hackers fruit farm at Coton is now a full-blown garden centre.

In Cambridge Dutch Elm disease opened up some new views of the colleges along the Backs, but outside town it left an already stark landscape even emptier.

In the 1960s some country lanes were surfaced with pale gravel chippings, giving a pleasantly rustic feel. The long straight and hummocky road from Girton to Madingley and the back route from Shelford to Newton were temporarily so blessed. Now they are the ubiquitous black tarmac, universally used by highways authorities. It is a shame too that most of the old rural signposts have gone, replaced with flat utilitarian models from an unstylish catalogue. Thank goodness that listing protects the sixteen milestones from Great St Mary's to Barkway, erected in 1728 under the will of Dr Mowse, Master of Trinity Hall, to mark the old coaching road to London. It's a good game to try to spot them all.

The force behind much of this change, direct or indirect, intended or unintended, has been the university. The new building programme, started so dramatically in the 1960s, has continued unabated. New colleges have been constructed, Robinson, Lucy Cavendish, Wolfson, Darwin, and virtually every teaching faculty has been rebuilt or extended. There are impressive new architectural statements to like or loath: Norman Foster's Law Faculty, close to Stirling's History building on the Sidgwick site, and described as a 'beached zeppelin of steel and glass';

King's Parade as it might have been. (Built Environment, 1972)

Ted Cullinan's Centre for Mathematical Sciences off Clarkson Road with its green roofs and ventilation cupolas; Michael Hopkin's Queen's Building at Emmanuel, a honey-coloured stone contrast to his Schlumberger tent; Eric Parry's elegant Foundress Court at Pembroke; the strikingly curvaceous Faculty of Education next to Homerton College and my old school, now the co-ed Hills Road Sixth-form College; the Jerwood Library for Trinity Hall by Freeland Rees-Roberts beside the Garret Hostel bridge, nicknamed 'The Ship on the Cam'. Among my favourites is Van Heyningen and Haward's Rare Books Library at Newnham, a striped-brick jewel box built in 1982.

On a much larger scale Giles Gilbert Scott's University Library has almost doubled in size with six phases of extensions, all to cater for the 100,000 books and 150,000 periodicals which it adds to its collection every year. The transformation of the Bankside power station into a new icon for London has elevated Scott's reputation, and the extensions in Cambridge are almost apologetically deferential.

One of my undergraduate friends and contemporaries at Jesus, Graham Morrison, has done more than most to augment Cambridge's building stock. Allies and Morrison have designed the Institute of Criminology and the Faculty of English, the Duke Building at Girton, the theatre and Gatehouse Court at Fitzwilliam, and the Rosalind Franklin Building at Newnham.

Some of the controversies of the 1960s now seem innocuous. At Queens' the Erasmus Building appears sedate compared to Cripps and Lyon Court, all gleaming white concrete, built in the 1980s across the river, west of the Mathematical Bridge, on the ancient Fellows' Garden and Grove wilderness. Lasdun's Brutalist shocker on King Street has been partly screened by

The 'armadilloo', Midsummer Common.

a three-storey lean-to extension, providing shops and offices and a respectable street frontage. The elevated status of Cambridge as a good place to live has inspired good new architecture in the town under the guidance of the City Planning Officers. The recent redevelopment of Bradwell's Court and Drummer Street is a distinct improvement. The Accordia development behind Brooklands Avenue has attracted award-winning architects such as Alison Brooks and Feilden Clegg Bradley, providing stylish flats and houses. The old single-storey government sheds and nuclear bunker have been replaced by smart new offices by Carey Jones Architects. Even the City Council have commissioned good schemes such as the eye-catching public toilets on Midsummer Common, nicknamed the 'armadilloo'.

Everyone has grown to like the West Road concert hall, while the old Music School in Downing Place, still with its blue double doors, is now part of the University Language Centre. West Road is now Cambridge's best venue for chamber music and small orchestras, famous for its performances by the resident Endellion String Quartet. I have played there many times, with London-based groups, or accompanying the Combined Village College Choirs (now the Cambridgeshire Choral Society), and enjoy its clear acoustics, good lighting and warmth. The make-over of Emmanuel Church in 1991 included a stage, new heating and generous lobbies, and is now a popular venue for concerts in the centre of town. Nobody much uses the old Guildhall now for music. Cambridge still lacks a large purpose-built symphony hall, and promoters still have to use King's Chapel, with its exhorbitant fees, or Ely Cathedral where woolly vests and long-johns are a necessity to combat the glacial temperatures.

Within the university the greatest expansion has been in postgraduate students, trebling between 1970 and 2008. There seems no limit to the amount of investment which Cambridge can attract for research. Bill Gates donated $210 million to create Gates postgraduate scholarships to study at Cambridge. Two Cambridge entrepreneurs gave £30 million to rename New Hall as Murray Edwards College. As the university celebrates its 800th birthday in 2009, its anniversary appeal, aiming to raise £1 billion by 2010, has already reached £700 million. There are some who talk now of concentrating solely on postgraduates; undergraduates are troublesome, often drunk, drugged and smelly, and most importantly don't make any money. Some have even suggested, perhaps tongue-in-cheek, that the Anglian Ruskin University, formerly the Cambridgeshire College of Arts and Technology and now proudly relaunched in modern premises in East Road, and the new Cambridge Regional College at Kings Hedges, could handle undergraduate requirements.

In 1969 the Mott Report recommended the expansion of science-based industries close to Cambridge and in 1970, Trinity College decided to develop their own land off Milton Road as a new science park. This huge site, beside the Northern bypass, and now home to over 100 high-tech firms, has been the biggest factor in the growth of the 'Cambridge Phenomenon' or 'Silicon Fen'. The university's own West Cambridge project alongside the Western bypass off Madingley Road will provide yet more. While Chivers Jam factory in Histon and Fisons at Hauxton have closed, they are not much mourned; thousands of people now work in new cleaner and better-paid research, development and manufacturing companies.

The transition from the austerity and insularity of Cambridge in the 1950s to the prosperity and opportunity of the last decade has been extraordinary. There can be nowhere in Britain where Harold Wilson's 'white heat of technology' has been more completely realised.

Thornton Way. No. 30 is on the right. (Airpic)

# GIRTON

In the summer of 1969, when I was between school and university, we moved house. My parents had been thinking about it for a while, spurred on by the increasing traffic on Histon Road and the burgeoning new estates in the vicinity. My father sometimes had to wait ten minutes for a gap in the traffic to get his car out of the drive in the morning rush-hour. With the co-operation of our neighbours in Roseford Road and permission from the local council, a separate small plot for a bungalow was created at the bottom of our garden, which added to the sale value. The house fetched £5,975, and the plot at the back £1,000. With the proceeds my parents could afford to go up the next rung of the property ladder and bought a smart post-war detached house in Thornton Way, Girton. Feeling less hard up and having resisted television while I was still at home, they now had enough spare cash to buy the latest Pye model, together with a fridge, toaster and washing machine, truly a white-goods bonanza.

The new house had a wider and deeper plot, but most importantly was in a no-through-road, part of a loop with Thornton Close, with no apparent proposals for change or development on the farmland beyond. As in Histon Road, the house had been built on former orchards and the long rear garden was well stocked with mature fruit trees, and backed onto the even bigger and well-wooded rear gardens of the distant houses on Thornton Close. Opposite was a row of police houses, rather mundane architecturally, but probably a bonus in terms of security and a deterrent to burglars. Given the long length of Thornton Road the house was sufficiently far from the busy Huntingdon Road to be free of traffic noise or vibration. As the crow flies it was only half a mile from our old house across the fields of the University Farm and the National Institute for Agriculture and Botany, but it was nearly three miles by road, and a much more salubrious neighbourhood. The immediate neighbours were the Birds, a retired city treasurer, and the Turners, also retired. Nothing much here was going to disturb the peace.

At the top of Thornton Way, near the corner where Thornton Road turns through ninety degrees and rises up to Girton Road, was a convenient parade of shops. Otherwise it was solidly residential, and solidly middle class. An old school friend of my mother's from Bedford, Barbara Booth, lived just round the corner in Thornton Close with her brainy husband Vernon who, as a sideline of his research into what makes a buttercup yellow, had published an influential book *Writing a Scientific Paper*. The Cubitts and the Hewitts from my parents' church lived in Thornton Road. Slowed down by a heart attack in 1970, my father took early retirement from the Great Ouse River Authority in 1974. On his index-linked government pension my parents were comfortably off and they happily settled into a quiet suburban existence. They even traded in their television for a 22in colour model, £370 from Darling & Wood in Cherry Hinton Road.

The historic centre of Girton village was nearly a mile away, along a road lined with straggling ribbon development, allotments and market gardens. One of these was Peter Graves' Oaklands Nursery, to which my mother quickly shifted her allegiance to buy flowers and foliage for her Sunday arrangements in Emmanuel Church. The spacious recreation ground became a good place to go with visiting grandchildren to play football or cricket and to collect conkers. Setting aside her non-conformist principles, my mother even started to help with the flower festival in the lovely old parish church of St Andrew. Despite the dreary suburban estates off Hicks Lane and Pepys Way, parts of the old village and the ancient thatched cottages of Duck End and Wood Green were surprisingly rural. Most of the fields and countryside around Girton were owned by Cambridge University Farm or the Animal Breeding Station, with more pasture and woodland than might have been the case with commercial arable farming. There were pleasant and well-maintained footpaths across meadows from the village to the Huntingdon Road, and the other side across the more wooded terrain to Madingley.

St Andrew's Church, Girton.

The Northern and Western bypasses and their vast spaghetti intersection changed all that in the late 1970s and cut a huge swathe through the Green Belt. Fortunately the Northern bypass and its continuation to the Bedford road was dug down into a cutting, mainly to protect the setting of the American Cemetery and Madingley Hall. Although it severed Girton College and Thornton Way from Girton village, with an ugly bridge on Girton Road, the excavation and embankments spared my parents' house from the worst traffic noise. Further west, hundreds of acres of the University Farm were gobbled up, the footpaths diverted or extinguished, and the tranquillity destroyed. The owners of the palatial houses along the west side of Huntingdon Road were not amused. Thorndyke, one of the last and greatest of Baillie Scott's Cambridge houses, had been set back behind a deep front garden to shelter the house from the old road. Now the rear, with its splendid two levels of dormer windows, was exposed to the M11 and the A14, and the constant roar of articulated lorries.

The spacious grounds of Girton College, with its woodland walk, its snowdrops, aconites and daffodils, and its beautifully kept playing fields, were now the best place for a pleasant stroll. From 1977 the famous women's college had started taking male students, in turn shedding its blue-stocking image and its ill-deserved reputation for remoteness ('more Cambridge students have visited Delhi than Girton' used to be the jibe). Bicycle lanes were created along Huntingdon Road. They certainly helped 'Snowy' (or Walter as he was really called) who cycled in on Saturdays from Oakington to Petty Cury with his menagerie of tame animals to raise money for charity.

The bypasses and the Science Park near Milton triggered fears that all the intervening land might be built on. That indeed may yet happen. The disused laundry and cold storage depot near the new bridge on Girton Road duly succumbed, and the oddly named 'Quills' housing estate now stretches behind the northern arm of Thornton Road, all bleached brick and garage courts. The university have so far desisted from building the long-threatened animal testing centre on Huntingdon Road, but in time surely the whole area across to Madingley Road will be built on. The fields beyond the hedge at the end of Thornton Way became set-aside, full of thistles and dock.

On a more positive note the creation in 2000 of Girton Wood as a Millennium project on the far side of the recreation grounds was a step in the right direction, only three hectares but the promise of more. The ten-hectare '800 Wood' on the University Farm's former arable land next to Madingley Wood is even more recent and ambitious, intended to have 15,000 new trees. They will provide some amelioration of the urban encroachment.

After my father died in 1991 I came back to Cambridge more regularly. His death had not been unexpected, plagued as he was with heart problems. Once when he had been sitting on his shooting-stick watching me cut the Lonicera hedge and talking to me about rugby or cricket, he said, 'When I die, be sure to look after your mother'. So I did, not that she needed much looking after. She had her widow's pension and my father's prudent savings. She was fit in mind and body and after years of caring and cooking for my father she was liberated to spend more time on her hobbies. She joined the Townswomen's Guild and the Girton Gardening Club, where she always won prizes in their summer show, as well as carrying on singing in the Cambridge Philharmonic Choir. In 2001 she took a solo role as a Gossip in three performance of Benjamin Britten's *Noye's Fludde*, not bad for an eighty-five-year-old. She frequently visited her favourite friends and relatives, her grandchildren in Hampshire, her cousin Margaret in Spalding, Pip and Buster in Stroud, and travelled on her own to North Carolina to stay with the Parrs, our old neighbours from Histon Road. Emmanuel Church and the garden in Thornton Way were her twin lynch-pins. Every other weekend I came back from London to help in the garden. Together we made improvements and refinements, extending the flower beds and herbaceous borders, planting a yew hedge and silver birch at the front. In the evenings I would visit my old school friend, John Richens, now back living in his parents' old house, where we would thrash through piano duets and then ride our bikes out to the Blue Ball in Grantchester for a pint.

And so it might have carried on to this very day. A few neighbours came and went, but most stayed put. The shops at the top of the Thornton Way occasionally changed hands, best of all when Chris Lloyd set up his bicycle business at No.2 in 1993. He was a real enthusiast, indeed still is, with a great collection of vintage bikes and spare parts, never at a loss to repair an old bone-breaker. With Chris' help, my mother's trusty Humber bicycle carried her around town, and her Renault 5, kept going by the garage on Huntingdon Road, took her further afield. She had the legs and heart to have lived as long and as healthily as her mother and grandmother.

# EPILOGUE

My mother's sudden death in a road accident on a sunny Friday afternoon in September 2003, on a country road just ten miles from my brother's house in Romsey, was a huge shock. Her body was taken from the mortuary in Winchester back to Cambridge, to Harry Williams' funeral parlour in Victoria Park, close to the Victoria Homes almshouses on Victoria Road where my mother had light-heartedly told me as a child that she might end up in her old age.

My mother had chosen Harry Williams when my father died. There, in the strange collection of extensions behind the house we had visited him, laid out in his coffin, his face suddenly looking thirty years younger, all the lines of pain and anxiety smoothed away. So now it was with my mother, and as she had done for my father, I went to Peter Graves' nursery to buy a single red rose for my final visit.

It had been a long hot summer, 100 degrees Fahrenheit at Heathrow in August, swelteringly hot, when I had been in Cambridge with my Cuban girlfriend for the second weekend in September. There had been a hosepipe ban, and the garden was dry and parched. Autumn was coming early. But before the funeral I ignored the ban, watered the lawns until they were green again and picked up every fallen leaf from the grass. The hearse brought the coffin back to Thornton Way and those neighbours who were not coming to the crematorium stood in silence by the road to mark their respect. Even the shopkeepers came out. Derek Wales returned to Cambridge to conduct the service of Thanksgiving in Emmanuel, which was packed with friends and relatives.

The *Cambridge Evening News* ran the story of my mother and also my father's wartime ordeal on a lifeboat, having been torpedoed on the SS *City of Nagpur* in the Atlantic in 1941 by the *U-75* German submarine. Among the condolences was a long letter from a man I'd never met who had shared that lifeboat, one of the 450 other survivors of the disaster.

For the rest of the autumn I continued to look after the garden with great devotion. I tried to remember to do all the things my mother had done: cutting back the blackberries, pruning the apple trees, dead-heading the roses, protecting the fuchsias against the early frosts, clearing the wild areas where my mother encouraged butterflies, and lighting bonfires to burn everything that could not be composted. I spread manure onto the beds and vegetable patch. The robin who had been an ever-present gardening companion of my mother, kept an eye on my work, picking up insects in my wake. I imagined that the tiny creature, so alert and attentive, was wondering where my mother had gone, even that the spirit of my mother was there within the robin itself.

By Christmas my brother and I had decided to sell the house. Neither of us wanted to live there; we didn't want to let it out; we couldn't afford to leave it empty just to go there for occasional weekends. As the slow regeneration began in the garden after the dark damp weeks of winter, I treasured every moment, the spring flowers and fruit blossom, the first crop of rhubarb. In April we helped to purchase a new grand piano for Emmanuel Church, as a memorial to my parents and to increase its potential as a concert venue.

We sold the house in May and completed in July. Over several exhausting weekends we cleared and cleaned the attic, the garage and outside shed, all those infrequently-opened cupboards and dusty top shelves. We came across a hundred memories, including boxes of old slides, some now printed on these pages. When we were finished and after my brother had set off back to Hampshire, I walked around the lawns for one last time and felt content that the garden was looking as my mother would have wanted. On that sunny Sunday evening as I finally closed the front door of the house, emptied of a lifetime's possessions, I knew that part of me was saying farewell to Cambridge.

Time, of course, waits for no man. Five years later, of my parents' generation, all those uncles and aunts, real and adopted, their friends and acquaintances, few now are still alive. Lorna, at ninety-five the oldest and pluckiest, has outlived them all. Tom Anderson, our doctor, died in 2003. Bridget Carmichael from the Perse Prep (always 'Miss' to me) died in 2005, so too from the senior school Malcolm MacFarlane, he of the bellowing voice on Sunday mornings, people indeed who might have enjoyed reading this book. Even poor old Snowy passed away in 2007, aged eighty-eight.

Within a few years of moving from Histon Road our old house had been altered out of recognition, the front garden paved over and an extension bigger than the original plonked on the side. So too with the house at Thornton Way, much has changed or disappeared, most sadly the copper beech in the back garden and the silver birch in the front which we had planted in memory of my father.

Last picture of my mother, with Varinia, in the back garden at Thornton Road, 14 September 2003.

The Corpus Clock.

In September 2008 Stephen Hawking unveiled an intriguing new public clock on the corner of Bene't Street and King's Parade. Designed by Dr John Taylor, formerly at Corpus, it features a giant mechanical grasshopper which munches the passing seconds and minutes, literally devouring time. It has become the latest 'place' in Cambridge for tourists to take photos of each other, but it might remind us too of our own mortality. Nothing, after all, is forever.